The Enhanced Role of Science Centres and Museums in Development Strategies

The Enhanced Role of Science Centres and Museums in Development Strategies

Proceedings of the
African Regional Conference,
Lusaka, Zambia
January 10-14, 2006

Editor
Vinay B. Kamble

CENTRE FOR SCIENCE & TECHNOLOGY OF THE
NON-ALIGNED AND OTHER DEVELOPING
COUNTRIES (NAM S&T CENTRE)
New Delhi, India

2008
DAYA PUBLISHING HOUSE
Delhi - 110 035

ISBN10 81-7035-523-0
ISBN13 978-81-7035-523-6
EAN: 9788170355236

Centre for Science and Technology of the Non-Aligned and Other Developing Countries (NAM S&T Centre)
Core-6A, 2nd Floor, India Habitat Centre, Lodhi Road,
New Delhi-110 003 (India)
Phone: +91-11-24644974, 24645134, Fax: +91-11-24644973
E-mail: namstct@gmail.com
Website: www.namstct.org

Supported by : **Vigyan Prasar**
A-50, Institutional Area, Sector 62,
Noida - 201 307 (U.P), India
Phone: +91-11-26967520, +91-120-2404438
Fax: +91-120-2404437
E-mail: info@vigyanprasar.gov.in
Website: www.vigyanprasar.gov.in

Published by : **Daya Publishing House**
1123/74, Deva Ram Park, Tri Nagar, Delhi - 110 035
Phone: 27383999, Fax: (011) 23260116
e-mail: dayabooks@vsnl.com
website: www.dayabooks.com
Showroom : 4760-61/23, Ansari Road, Darya Ganj
New Delhi - 110 002
Phone: 23245578, 23244987

Laser Typesetting : **Classic Computer Services**
Delhi - 110 035

Printed at : **Chawla Offset Printers**
Delhi - 110 052

Printed in India

Preface

This Volume includes presentations made by the participants at the African Regional Conference organized at Lusaka on Enhanced Role of Science Centres and Museums in Development Strategies during the period 10-14 January 2006. Most of the individuals are working, or have at one time or another worked in a science centre or a museum. Most of the presentations, therefore, deal with exhibits, programmes and strategies to attract more visitors and engage them in meaningful activities related to understanding of scientific phenomena and application of science and technology in day-to-day life. A common thread running in the presentations is the role the science centres and museums play to act as a bridge between the people and the R&D labs from where new technologies flow; and explain their possible impact on the environment and society. Indeed, science centres and science museums are the nuclei where begins a process of transformation of a country into a nation of scientifically minded people.

There is no gainsaying the fact that the level of science and technology communication and popularization in different countries that participated in the workshop exhibits significant variation. Countries like India and South Africa have museum networks which are very well developed, while there are countries trying to catch up with the rest of the world. In any case, there has been a growing consciousness among the developing countries about the role played by science centres and museums in educating the people and in the improvement of the quality of life. Efforts of NAM S&T Centre are, therefore, noteworthy in bringing together science popularization experts and museologists from the developing countries on a common platform to share their knowledge and experiences. It is hoped that the present Volume would be of immense utility in initiating and sustaining people's science movements in developing countries.

As one would expect the writing styles and the idioms employed by the authors exhibit wide variation. Hence, editing this Volume turned out to be a relatively uphill task. Occasionally, I have taken liberties and made minor alterations in order to make the presentations more readable. In the process, I do hope I have not earned the ire of the authors. If so, I express my sincere apologies to them.

Vinay B. Kamble
Director, Vigyan Prasar

Contents

Introduction

Science centres and museums are the gateway to the curiosity and interests in science for common people of all ages. A visit to these places gives a first hand familiarity and opportunity to closely perceive the natural world. These are the modern 'temples' where one can discover, explore and test ideas about the physical world and as such they represent the resources for informal learning. Their location at a special nexus among the community, the school and the home provides them a unique role in the educational infrastructure, one that can propel science education and other developmental reforms into the 21st century. These can be the asylum connecting individuals and families and offering opportunity to raise public awareness of current research, providing a neutral venue for debate and dialogue, and stimulating an interest in science among young people.

The role of the science centres and museums in developing countries has expanded to forge a more confident relationship between science and society. Developing countries in recent years have been experiencing unparalleled advancement of science and technology. Since the visual impression aids facilitate the process of quickly grasping various facets of any new knowledge, these entities play a pivotal role in comprehending these developments and their impact on the socio-economic progress, particularly in emerging economies. Various strategies can be hatched and developed by keeping in mind the personal, societal, economic and political values that science centres and museums would offer if supported. The arena where these can be of importance in development of society on the whole are local / regional / international tourism, youth employment, community partnerships, volunteer schemes, urban redevelopment, environment restoration, and impact on government policies and priorities that can be designed and reframed for better exploitation and ensuring sustainable development. To support the right policies in the fields of science and technology, people should be involved in the debate on the social and ethical issues raised by new technologies. Science centres and museums can be successful places for such debates because they help visitors to meet science in a friendly and interactive environment and also because they play a neutral role, giving a voice to the different opinions.

Due to the great importance of science education and popularisation of science and technology in the society at large, the Centre for Science and Technology of the Non-Aligned and Other Developing Countries (NAM S&T Centre) has been organizing a series of international and regional level workshops and conferences on this aspect. Beginning with an international workshop on 'The Role of Science Centres in Development Strategies' held in Kolkata, India in Nov.-Dec. 2002, the Centre organized the 1st Knowledge Fest and 2nd International Forum and Workshop for Culture of Science, Technology and Innovation in Society in Bogotá, Colombia in partnership with the Maloka Science Centre of Colombia during March 2004 as a regional workshop for the Latin American and Caribbean countries; an international workshop on the theme: 'The Changing Role of Science Centres and Museums in Developing Countries' at Hanoi, Vietnam in collaboration with the Center for Regional Research & Development (CRD) in October 2004; and the 2nd regional workshop titled 'African Regional Conference on Enhanced Role of Science Centres and Museums in Development Strategies' at Lusaka, Zambia during 10–14 January, 2006 jointly with the National Science Centre of Zambia. Twenty five scientists and senior experts from 8 countries, which included Angola [Mr. Emmanuel Jeronimo Jaime João Chitende, Angolan Embassy in Zambia], Botswana [Mrs. Gloria Tiny Seitei, Senior Communications Officer, Botswana Technology Centre, Gaborone], India [Dr. Tapan K. Ganguly, Director, Science City, Kolkata and Dr. Abhay Kothari, Manthan, Ahmedabad], Japan [Mr. Hideo Nakano, Senior Volunteer, JICA], Pakistan [Dr. Mrs. Alia Bano Munshi, Principal Scientific Officer, PCSIR Complex, Karachi], South Africa [Dr. Richard Waller, Greenhouse Management Services, Johannesburg and Mr. Alfred Tsipa, President SAASTEC and Manager, Unizul Science Centre, Empangeni], Sri Lanka [Mr. Arumahennadige Piyasiri, Mechanical Engineer, National Engineering Research and Development Centre, Ja-ela] and Zambia [Mr. John S. Muyangana, Principal Education Officer, Mrs. Hilda L. Nyemba, Mr. Donald K. Mwaba and Mr. James M. Chongo, Senior Education Officer and other officials of the National Science Centre; Mr. George S. Mudenda, Director, Lusaka National Museum; and participants representing the Ministries of Education and Science & Technology] attended this last event and technical papers and status reports on the activities related to the science centres and museums in their respective countries were presented by them during the African regional conference at Lusaka.

The present publication is primarily a compilation of the presentations made during the Lusaka workshop. I am thankful to Dr. T. Ramasamy, Vice-President NAM S&T Centre and Secretary to the Government of India, Department of Science & Technology (DST) and to Vigyan Prasar, the premier autonomous organization under DST for the popularisation of science for support in bringing out this publication. I am particularly grateful to Dr. Vinay B. Kamble, Director, Vigyan Prasar and Advisor, DST, for undertaking to edit this publication. Last, but not the least, I acknowledge the dynamic involvement of the entire team of the NAM S&T Centre, in particular, Mr. M. Bandyopadhyay, Mr. Gaurav Gaur, Ms. Priyanka Ahuja and Mr. Pankaj Buttan in compiling the presented papers and giving a shape to the volume.

I sincerely trust that this publication will impart excellent technical material for the readers, serving as a valuable reference material for the professionals working on science education, particularly related to science popularisation, science centres and science museums, and will help the developing countries in working out appropriate strategies and programmes for the development and exploitation of science centres and museum for using them to benefit the society.

(Arun P. Kulshreshtha)
Director, NAM S&T Centre

Challenges of Establishing a Science Centre in a Developing Country: A Case Study Based on Botswana's First Science Centre - The Discovery Centre

Gloria Tiny Seitei
Botswana Technology Centre, Botswana
E-mail: Gloria@botec.bw

Abstract

This paper outlines the experiences of the Botswana Technology Centre in establishing the first science centre in Botswana called the Discovery Centre. It starts by discussing project concept, consultation process with stakeholders, approach used to acquire the exhibits, trial run, marketing and evaluation exercise done six months after commissioning of the facility.

The results of the monitoring and evaluation of the project are a major component of this paper. The main purpose of the monitoring exercise was to assess the impact of visits and to find out if the Centre was achieving its objectives or not from the different visitor groups. Another aim of the evaluation was to determine the acceptance level of the Centre by the target audience.

The evaluation was conducted through administering of a questionnaire to visitors as they exit after interacting with all the exhibits. Teachers/instructors and parents accompanying groups on their visit also completed the questionnaire and provided more information via an unstructured interview. In addition, the results indicate that visit to the centre provided entertainment/enjoyment and educational value to most visitors.

The preliminary findings of the monitoring and evaluation are that majority of visitors have expressed appreciation of the services rendered at the Centre and some of them would like to make repeat visits in future.

The evaluation exercise has also established that visitors have diverse interests in terms of their preferences and reasons for their visits to the centre. Factors influencing such differences in preferences include age, gender, education geographic location of potential visitors and their profession.

The results of evaluation have also identified challenges such as lack of access to information, lack of money to pay for transport costs, location of the centre and staffing situation. Facilities such as exhibition space, rest area, ablution and lecture room also needs to be taken into account.

Key words: Science and technology; science centres; evaluation; interviewees; exhibits; exhibition; interactive

Background: History of the Discovery Centre

The project concept started in April 1999 as a Technology on Wheels with the aim of promoting science and technology (S&T) in the country through use of mobile science museums. The project was to involve a mobile trailer containing science exhibits towed by a vehicle to travel to different places across the country.

In 17th November 1999, after consultation with the Ministry of Finance and Development Planning, it was decided that the concept was not viable as it required high capital investment of purchasing a truck and a trailer that were not going to be used most of the time hence the project was taken back to the drawing board.

In 2000/2001 consultation with stakeholders and experts involved in science centres. As a result of this process, a new project concept was formulated that resulted in the National Science, Engineering and Technology Exploratorium (NSETE) now known as the Discovery Centre.

On 30th April 2001 submission of project memorandum was made to the Ministry of Finance and Development Planning with a budget of P 2 400 000 (US$ 506 879). This was then followed by a project memorandum on 27th June 2001 which was approved by the Ministry of Finance and Development Planning to cover costs for consultancy and supply of exhibits. On 21st March 2002 advertisements were placed in the media (newspapers and Internet) inviting tenders locally and internationally for the supply and installation of interactive exhibits.

On 22nd October 2002 the tender was awarded to Exhibition Services company in Australia and a contract of agreement was signed on 21st May 2003 between Botswana Technology Centre and Exhibition Services for design, fabrication and supply of interactive science exhibits.

2nd - 16th June 2004 saw the installation and testing of exhibits at the Discovery Centre. These were then signed off and approved by BOTEC on 1st - 30th June 2004. After testing and approval of exhibits a trial run followed on 1st-30th November 2004, and was opened to the public on 2nd February 2005.

Rationale

The Discovery Centre is the first science centre in Botswana and there are few people in this country who have visited science centres in other parts of the world. This means that majority of the people including the staff of the Discovery Centre have limited knowledge and experience about science centres. Secondly it is difficult to establish a benchmarking strategy as there are no similar facilities in Botswana. The purpose of the monitoring and evaluation exercise was to assess the successes and failures of the facility. Data collection was done from 22/06/05 to 30/09/05.

The objectives of the monitoring and evaluation exercise were:

- To assess if the Discovery Centre is achieving its main objectives or not.
- To determine the acceptance level of the facility by the target audience.
- To identify technical and administrative factors which are likely to affect the successful implementation of the project.
- To assess if the resources for the Centre are adequate or not
- To identify how best stakeholders could be involved in the activities of the Centre.
- To make recommendations on the way forward

The main purpose of this report is to analyse data obtained from the monitoring and evaluation exercise, then make conclusions and recommendations on the way forward.

Four consultative meetings with stakeholders were held before tendering and acquisition of exhibits.

First Consultation Meeting with Stakeholders (31/05/2001)

The purpose of this meeting was to explain the concept of the Discovery Centre and to brainstorm on themes that would be used in deciding on list of exhibits. Participants in the meeting were also given an opportunity to share amongst themselves key issues in their areas of operation. The purpose of discussing key issues was to ensure that themes suggested for the centre would be relevant to the needs of Botswana. Key issues were identified as follows:

- Difficult scientific concepts
- Lack of knowledge on using apparatus and equipment
- Teachers not involved when new equipment are purchased
- No access to catalogues for school apparatus
- No in-service training for teachers on science subjects
- Lack of appreciation on application of mathematics to real life problem solving
- Need to review school syllabuses in science subjects
- The problem of territorial systems in education.
- Science and Gender
- Science and Society
- Promotion of indigenous materials
- Language
- Lack of SET apparatus in Primary schools and Pre-Schools

Second Consultation Meeting with Stakeholders (22/08/2001)

The purpose of the meeting was to consolidate themes suggested in the first meeting of stakeholders and to develop a priority list. A member of SAASTEC facilitated the meeting. At the end of the meeting, more than 50 themes and a list of about 200 exhibits was suggested. Due to time pressure, it was not possible to finalise the priority list of themes and exhibits, hence it was decided to call the third stakeholders meeting.

Third Stakeholders Meeting (Last week of September)

The purpose of this meeting was to finalise the themes and list of exhibits for the Discovery Centre. The meeting decided on 13 themes and 62 exhibits. BOTEC was given a mandate to decide on the final list of themes and exhibits.

Final list of themes and exhibits

After further consultation with experts and some suppliers, a priority list of themes and exhibits was finalised as follows:

THEME	EXHIBIT
Biology	Human torso
	HIV Roulette
	Giant microscope
Physics	Newton's cradle
	G-Force
	Fibre optics
Transport and communications	Whispering dishes
	Snooping funnel
	Combustion engine
	Broadcasting
	Driving simulation
Geography	Aeolian landscape
	Tornado
Cosmology	Blast off
	Telescope
Water	Running water
Environment	Stream table

Consultations with Experts

The main aim of this consultation process was to learn the best practices from experts. Consultation methods included, study visits, internet searches and literature searches.

Acquisition of Exhibits:

Purchase from local or regional suppliers

Local or regional contractors will lead to cost advantages, on-site assistance, real-time guarantees and local circumstances will be taken into account. Models could be customised for a better fit in the planned centre. Difficulties will be in finding a capable, reliable and available contractor who will be prepared to invest time and effort in developing, prototyping and producing one-off items. Another disadvantage is that it takes longer to acquire exhibits than off-the-shelf models.

Designing and constructing own models

This is the most cost effective way of procuring models. However, it requires a dedicated team of capable and experienced people who can combine their expertise, knowledge, skills and experience to produce models of an acceptable standard. The emphasis here is on a dedicated team. What does not work is making use of an organisation's available 'capacity' on an ad-hoc or 'begging' basis. It goes without saying that the necessary on-site facilities will have to be available as well as suppliers of specialised materials, parts and equipment.

Outright purchase (off-the-shelf models)

This is the swiftest option but most expensive way of getting started. Models are selected and purchased from abroad. Shipping, insurance and importation duties add to the total cost. Time delays in getting the models should be taken into account. Air freight delivery could amount to 60% or more of the cost of the model depending on its weight and size. Any warranty repairs will have to be reshipped to the supplier. It is also difficult to provide back-up support, on-site guarantees and training of staff by the supplier.

Exhibits and Services:

Indoor exhibits

These are exhibits that are considered to be delicate such that they cannot withstand hash environment such as rain, ultraviolet light from the sun or dust and they are also generally small in size hence it is safer to keep them in a secure place where they can be protected by security officers 24 hours a day.

Outdoor exhibits

Criteria for selecting out door exhibits are factors such as robust and large sizes that may no fit inside the building. Materials used for building outdoor exhibits should be resistant to erosion, ultraviolet light and strong enough to allow visitors to interact with them without breakages.

Demonstration or Lecture Room

A careful selection of topics that teachers consider to be difficult to teach to students in schools are usually demonstrated in lecture rooms. Stakeholders in particular, teachers as well as other technical professionals have to be involved in selecting topics that will form part of demonstrations.

Road shows or mobile unit

The idea was to extend the services of the centre to other parts of the country by transporting some exhibits in a vehicle and displaying them in places outside Gaborone.

Other services that are part of this offer include the following:

- Provision of labelled text to suit target audiences.
- Resource Centre - Science books, videos, DVD's, science magazines, etc.
- Workshops – Maintenance and fabrications of exhibits
- Tuck-shops – Sell snacks, science promotional toys / gadgets to visitors
- Training of staff on daily operations of the centre.

Methodology for Data Collection

Design of a survey instrument

The design of the survey instrument was started by identifying and selecting variables that are relevant to the objectives of the study as stated in the rationale. The following variables were selected:

- Gender
- Age of visitors
- Distance from the Discovery Centre
- Level of education
- Profession of visitors
- Level of appreciation of the facility
- Mode of transport
- Reasons for visiting the Discovery Centre
- Length of visits
- Exhibits preferred
- Sources of information (Media)

These variables were later used as a basis for designing a survey instrument. There were no decisions made on specific indicators for these variables.

Effort was put in to ensure that questions were framed such that they were mutually exclusive. Some questions were used to get the expressed opinions of respondents. Other questions were based on multiple choice answers where respondents simply selected the relevant answers from a given number of choices. There was only one open-ended question to allow respondents to state their views on some aspects of the facility.

Data collection methods

The guiding principle was to select data collection techniques that involved participation of visitors to the Centre. The emphasis was placed on simple techniques that yield practical results relatively quick. The two techniques that were selected and used for data collection were observation and administering a written questionnaire. The dialogue technique involved noting comments, questions and remarks made by visitors. The dialogue technique was necessary to capture some of the information that was not catered for in the questionnaire. It also catered for a situation where interviewees may forget or be unwilling to write certain things in the questionnaire. The dialogue technique allows researches to test the reliability of responses from interviewees.

The study mainly used structured questionnaire as it is easy to do quantitative analysis of data and to administer given the limited human resource. The questionnaire was made up of fixed questions in a standard sequence with fixed answers. There was only one open-ended question. The interviewees completed questionnaires on their own and handed them to the reception desk before their departure.

Sampling method

At the end of the tour, some of the visitors were randomly selected to complete questionnaires. The number of visitors who completed the questionnaires was 410 out of a total 1867. This gives a sample size of 410/1867 or 22%. This is a satisfactory representative percentage.

Data Analysis

Previous visits to the Centre

The interviewees were asked if they had visited the Centre before or not. 80% responded that it was their first visit to the Centre while only 11% of them had visited the Centre before. This was expected as the Discovery Centre was only opened to the public in February 2005. Within this short period only small percentage of the visitors would have had a chance to visit the Centre for more than once. 9% did not answer the question.

Length of visit to the Centre

Majority of people (58%) did not respond to the question on 'How long did you spend at the Centre?" 24% of the respondents said 2 – 4 hours while 16% said 1 – 2 hours. This means that future visits to the Centre could be planned to last for an average of 3 hours.

How long did you spend at the centre

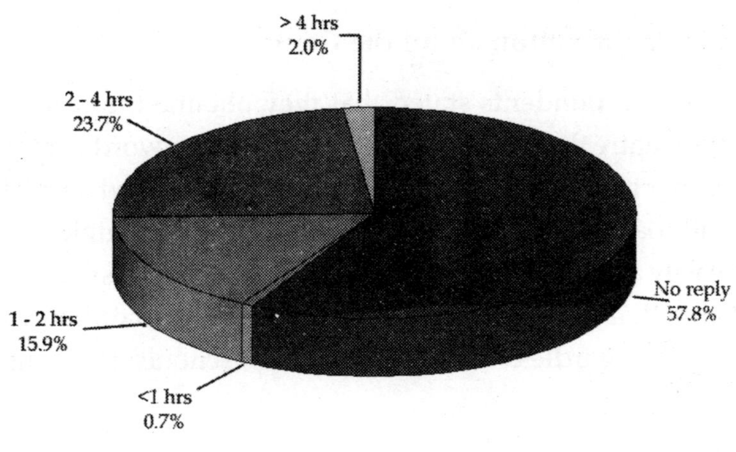

Purpose of the visit

Majority of visitors (67%) came to the Centre either to see new exhibits or to see special exhibition show. Only 19% of the visitors did not state their main reasons for visiting the Centre. This means that majority of visitors were adventurers with the main interest of exploring the world (i.e. to be the first to see new things).

What are the main reasons for your visit?

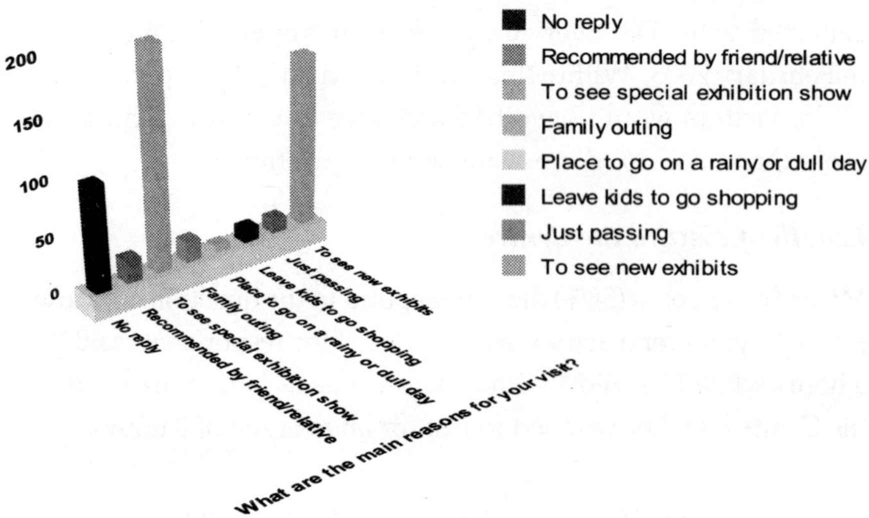

Source of Information about the Centre

Most of the respondents stated that they obtained information about the Centre through radio (21%) followed by word of mouth (13%). Other important sources of information included television news and road signs. This means that radio is still a single media that is easily accessible to majority of the people in Botswana. It is interesting that even schools regard radio as their main source of information regardless of letters sent to all schools as means of communication.

How did you hear about the Discovery Centre

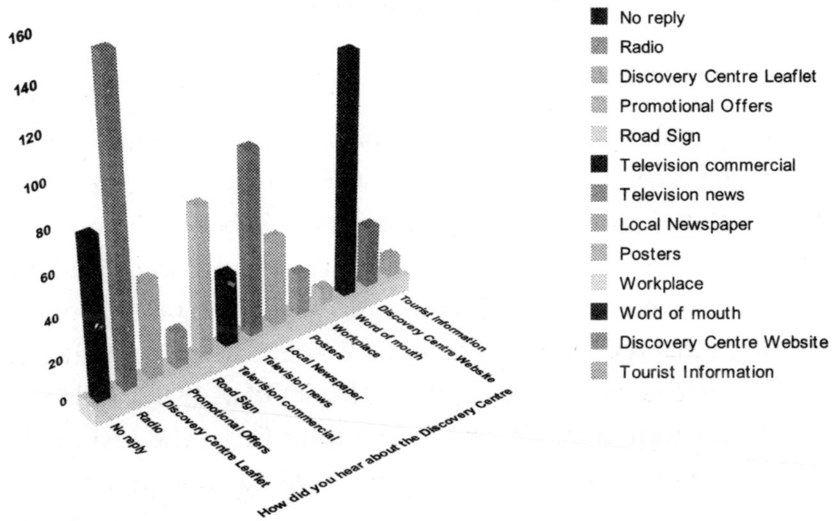

Future visits to the Centre

Most of the respondents (87%) stated that they would like to visit the Centre again in future. It is not clear as to why they would like to visit the Centre again. May be a follow up question would have helped to reveal their reasons. This could mean that they did

Would you like to visit the Discovery Centre again?

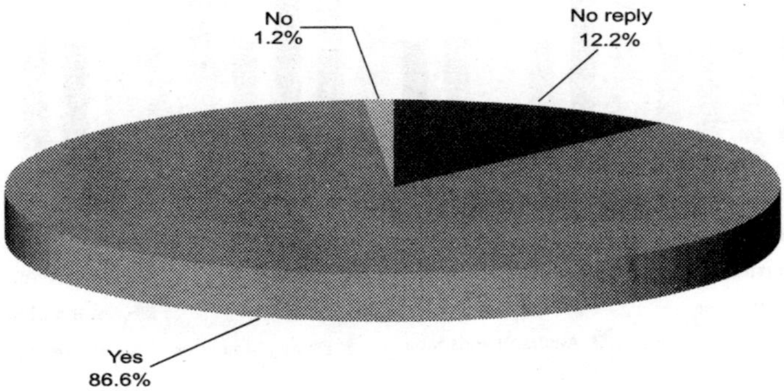

not have enough time to interact with exhibits. It could also mean that the exhibits helped them to understand scientific concepts learned in schools, hence they believe that future visits would further reinforce the knowledge gained on their first visit.

Preferred exhibits

The overall rating about satisfaction of visitors to the Centre mainly ranged between good and excellent (67%) and only 2% of the visitors stated a low level of satisfaction (i.e. between poor and very poor).The most popular exhibit was the driving simulator which was rated between good and excellent by 82.2% of the visitors, followed by G-Force at 81.7% and Running Water at 80.3%.The least popular exhibit was Blast Off at 48.8%, followed by Planetarium at 52.2% and Tornado at 58%. The rest of the exhibits ranged between 60% and 80%. On the other hand when

If so which attractions?

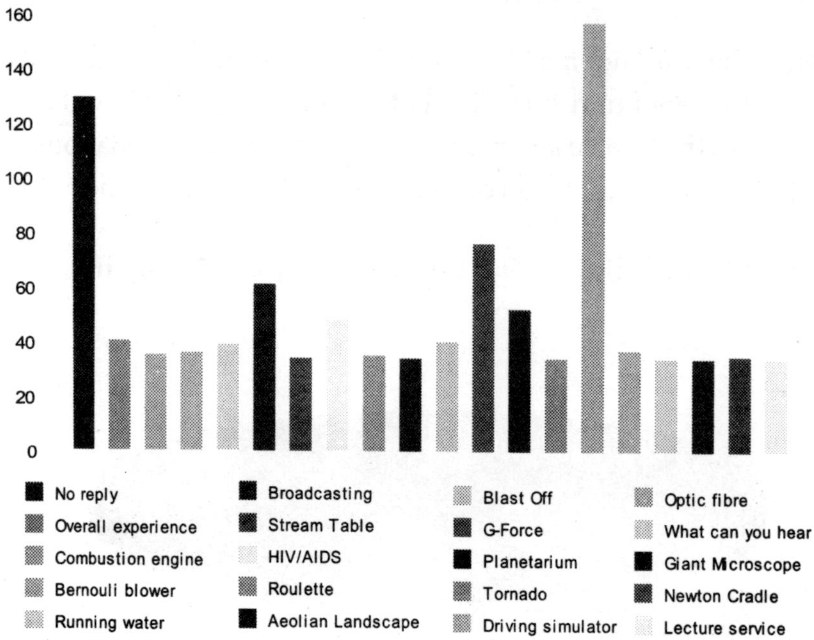

the scores for poor and very poor ratings were used, Combustion engine was the least popular exhibit at a score of 12.2% followed by Aeolian Landscape. HIV Roulette and Driving Simulator both scored 1.2% under poor and very poor. The rest scored between 1.7% and 3.9%.

In stating their satisfaction level for each exhibit most of the respondents (39%) did not grade the Blast Off, followed by Planetarium at 36.9% and Snooping funnel at 25.3%. Both the blast-off and the planetarium were not in operation during the survey due to some mechanical problems. Exhibits with non respondent to this question were G-Force at 11.9% and Driving Simulator at 11.2%. The rest of the exhibits ranged between13.1% and 23.2%.

Reasons for being attracted to exhibits

Out of a total of 410 interviewees, 121 of them did not comment or give reasons on why they were attracted to some of the exhibits and not to others. The remaining interviewees made comments that scored as follows;

Educational and learning	69
Learn how to drive	48
Fun and interesting	15
Good and useful	14

One interesting point noted was that driving simulator came up clearly as the most popular exhibit. In fact some of the interviewees stated categorically that, 'driving simulator is more fun than others'. There were other comments that confirmed that the Centre is achieving its objective of promoting SET through edutainment. Examples of these comments were; it is fun, it is interesting, it is educational and I want to learn more about science.

Mode of transport

Most of the visitors (80%) were students who came to the Centre on school visits using either Government transport or vehicles hired by schools. About 10% of the respondents did not state the mode of transport they used to visit the Centre. 4.1% used cars, 0.5% cycled and 0.2% walked.

Age group

About 76% of visitors were of the age 10 – 14 years. This age group is made up of students in junior secondary schools and upper classes in primary schools. There were no visitors from senior secondary schools as exhibits do not cover chemistry and biology demonstrations in the BGCSE school syllabus. Only 6% of the visitors were 25 years old and above (i.e. adults). These figures

Which age group are you in?

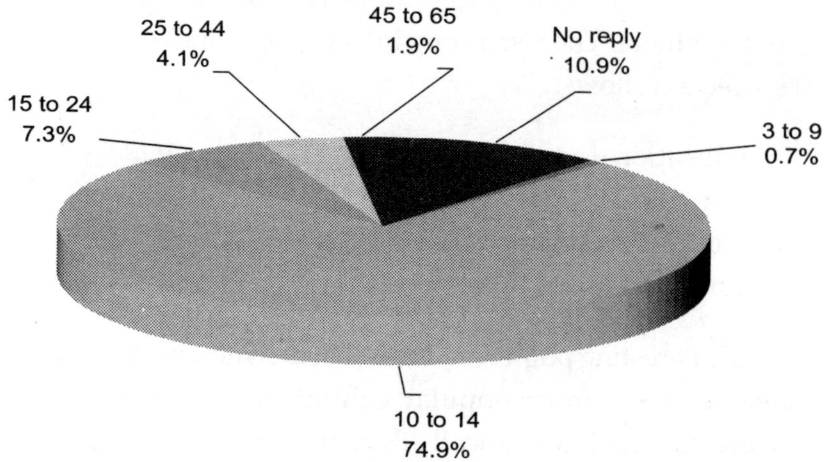

confirmed that the ideal target audience of the Centre is mainly junior secondary schools and this is common in most of the science centres around the world.

Gender

Majority of visitors were females (48%) while males were only 33%. This seems to contradict the general perception that males have more interest in science subjects than females. In fact most of SET professions in Botswana are dominated by males. The main explanation for these seemingly unusual results is that the number of females includes mothers who accompanied their young children (i.e. pre-school).

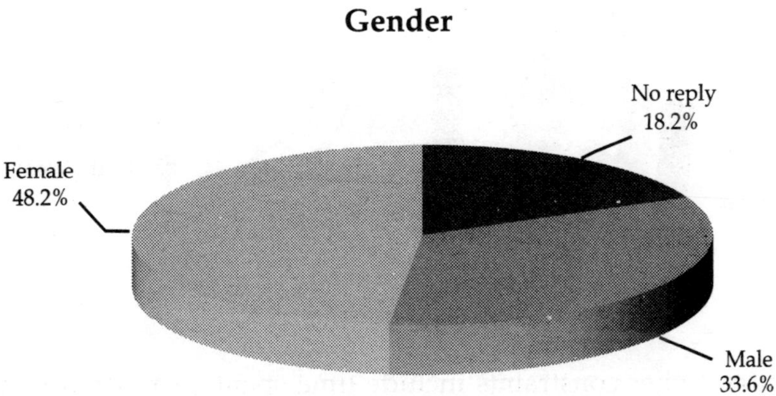

Geographical location

Majority of visitors (38.5% were from Gaborone followed by Kgatleng District (18.3%), Central District (9.3%) Kweneng District (8.8%) and South East District (6.8). On the other hand, Kgalagadi District had only 0.2% of visitors and North West District had 0.7%. This means that the further away the people are located from Gaborone the less number of them are able to visit the Discovery Centre. This could be understood in the sense that the longer the distance the place is located away from the Discovery Centre, the higher the transport cost. This huge transport cost is unaffordable to most of the schools and individuals particularly in the rural areas hence very few of them managed to visit the

How far do you live from the Discovery Centre?

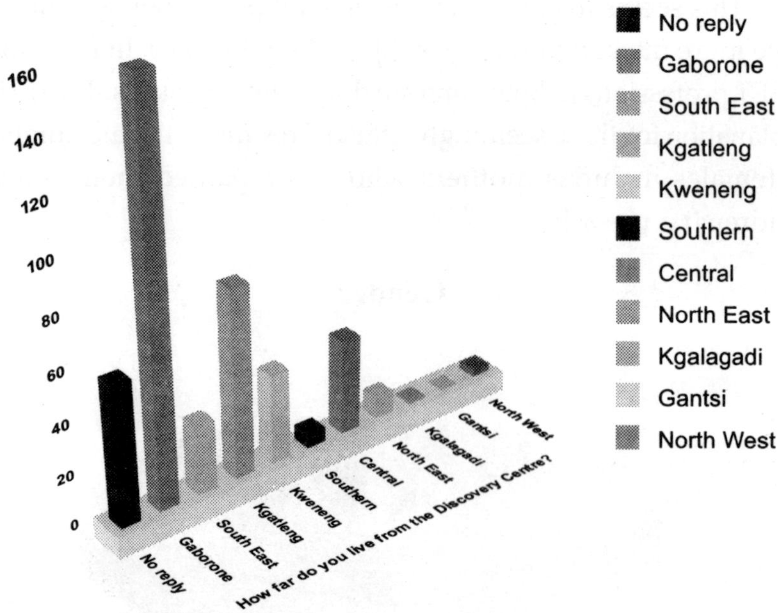

Centre. Other constraints include time spent away from home and cost of living expenses during the trip.

Communication

The table below shows that only 4 respondents or 1% of the 410 interviewees had access to electronic mail. This is due to the fact that the visitors were mostly students who did not have means to own hardware and software equipment associated with Internet services. This means that e-mail cannot be used as part of the communication strategy for promoting the Centre. The second point noted from the table is that 79 (19.3%) of interviewees stated that they did not have any means of communication. This means that it is not possible for BOTEC to communicate directly with about 20% of the potential visitors to the Centre. This table also shows that the three common means of communication are

	Mode of communication	Number of visitors
1	E-mail	4
2	Telephone/mobile	273
4	Postal address	140
5	Postal and telephone/mobile	83
7	Fax	6
9	No response	79

telephone, mobile phone and postal address. Fax was only used by six people. All these six people had access to telephone, mobile phone and postal addresses.

Weekly visits

The table below shows that the Discovery Centre had the highest number of visitors on the third week of September, followed by the second week of August and third week of August. September received the highest number of visitors followed by August as the school vacation was during these two months. The Centre received the lowest number of visitors due to the fact that the evaluation covered the last two weeks of this month.

Month	Week 1	Week 2	Week 3	Week 4	Week 5	Total
June	0	0	0	25	147	172
July	0	3	148	71	140	362
August	96	229	196	124	12	657
September	3	3	638	172	0	816
Total						2007

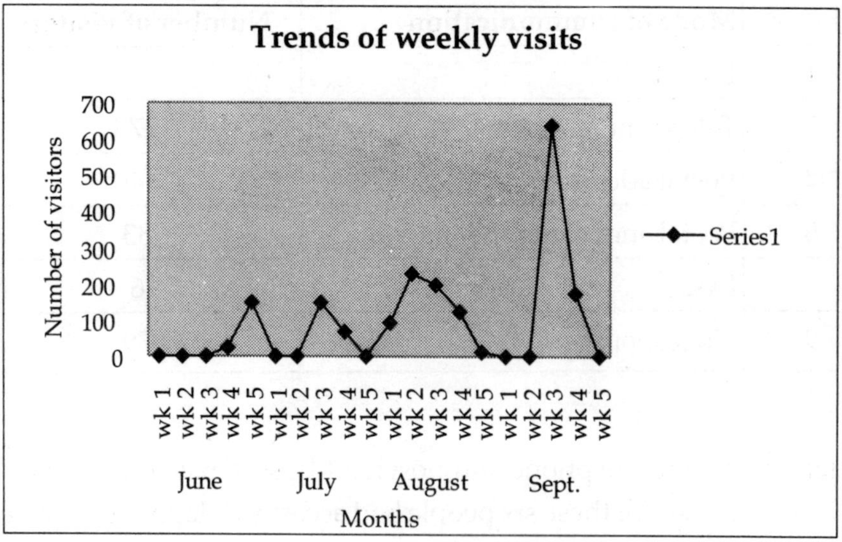

Profession

Majority of visitors (85%) were students. About 15% of the visitors did not state their professions. This 15% includes mothers, teachers, researchers, Government employees, pre-school kids, the general public and other professionals.

Information dissemination

Majority of visitors would like to receive information on organising a group visit (35%) and topics for lectures (30%). Very few visitors (10%) expressed interest to receive information on corporate hospitality. About 24% of visitors did not state the type of information they would like to receive from the Centre.

General conclusion

For as long as the Discovery Centre uses the rented facility at International Commerce Park with its current setup it is not practically possible to attract visitors or break even. Based on this understanding, we recommend that under the current situation,

Which of the following would you like to receive further

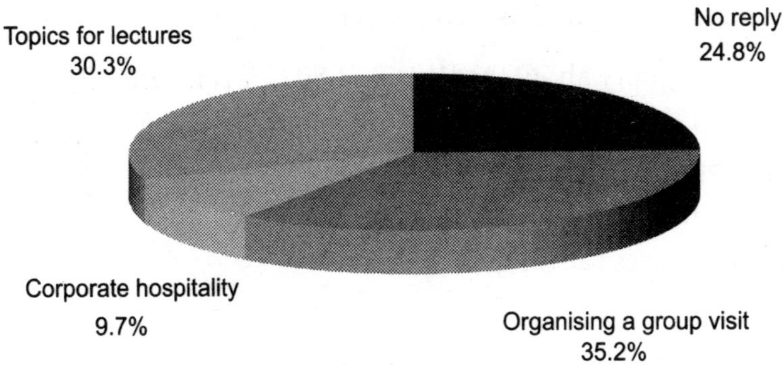

BOTEC should not aim to run the Centre on a cost recovery basis. It should simply be viewed as a long term investment for the country that will contribute towards public knowledge on science and technology related issues. It should also be seen as a BOTEC project and not a departmental project hence all the skills of the organization should be pooled together to ensure its success e.g. marketing.

Feedback from visitors

The Centre is located in the commercial area and not in the public place hence it is not suitable for students/public

- The location of the Discovery Centre is isolated during weekends and is also not secure for visitors coming to the Discovery Centre.
- Clients are complaining that the area is not conducive in terms of accessibility and poor transport system especially during weekends.
- There is no rest and eating area for students/public. This has proved to be a problem particularly during rainy days.

- The structure is not suitable for larger groups. For example the toilets are few and not suitable for larger groups. This has also been cited as a concern by visitors.
- Visitors query about the P10.00 (1.80 US$) entrance fee. They feel that since the Discovery Centre is a government sponsored facility, entrance fee should not be charged from the visitors.

The Enhanced Role of Science Centres and Museums in Developing Strategies

Nikola Rizk Guirgues
General Director,
City of Science, Academy of Scientific Research and Technology, Egypt
E-mail: rizknikola@yahoo.com

Abstract

In order to enhance role of Science Centres and Museums in developing strategies, the significant criteria identified are as follows:

Exhibits, that are beautiful even funny - can encourage visitors to approach new phenomena, show evolution of science, try to give a better understanding to the world of science, nature and technology show science as integral part of culture, and exemplify its relation to daily life and the exhibits which deals with subjects like : optics, liquids, mechanics, electricity etc. are designed for interaction, using the"hands on" museum style.

The Children's Discovery Museum is a creative and challenging interactive experience, fostering curiosity and encouraging children to explore the wonders of science, to ask questions, and then allow them to learn through guided play and exploration.

Laboratories where activities and experiments take place in many scientific subjects such as: chemistry, physics, optics, electricity, physiology etc.

Libraries: Museums should encourage to allow children read simple scientific books.

Environment: Museums should encourage to learn environment, how to keep environment clean from pollution (water, air and earth).

Computer: Museums should encourage to use computers in everyday life.

The internet: Museums should encourage to use the internet to gather information and connect with other museums by using museum websites.

Learning languages: The learning of English language should be encouraged to accelerate learning by accessing important world websites.

Partnerships between Museums and Schools: Museum professionals need to explore strategies, models, and structures that can facilitate more meaningful relationships between schools and museums, in which :

- There would be an understanding and appreciation of the museum as a learning environment with multiple outcomes.
- The concept of " learning" would be shared across both environments, that is schools and museums.
- There would be an awareness that museums can be used in multiple ways , beyond conventional formats or models, such as field trips or teacher professional development.

- The experiences that result from the collaboration between museums and schools would be negotiated among all parties – teacher, students, parents, and museums educators.
- The museum would be viewed not only as learning environment, but as an organization that supports, facilitates, and enhances specific types of learning.
- Students would see the museums as a unique environment, supporting lifelong learning.

Scientific Trips, museums should encourage scientific trips to learn about scientific environments in nature.

Publications, to spread simple scientific culture need simple scientific books and other form of publications.

Scientific Research, museums should encourage to carry out scientific research in association with agencies to provide a better understanding of the positive role of museums in contemporary society.

Lectures, museums should encourage scientific lectures on different branches of science (physics, chemistry, geology, etc.).

Museums should encourage inventor's workshop, for example carpentry, helping build a boat, or a car, or do fun sculpture. Use imagination, construct something interesting and take it home.

Keywords: Science Museums - Exhibits - The Children's Discovery Museum - Science Education - Laboratories - Environment - Science Libraries - Scientific Research

Introduction

The quantity of information, flowing mainly through mass media such as the press, radio and television, has been constantly growing.The importance of these media for education is unquestionable. In view of the fact that the people are generally overdosed with verbal information; the hands-on experience has acquired particular importance.

This is where museums, possessing genuine material, pictorial and otherwise, come to play an important role. They make it possible to acquire knowledge through sensory perception of an object - a source of information - and, a direct contact with natural phenomena and appreciation of historical events. Besides, the effect of museum exhibits on man is increased many times over by the emotional factors which, as psychology has proved, play a major role in cognition and personality formation. An example that is universally recognized is the incomparable effect on man of genuine works of art and commemorative objects connected with great events or great personalities.

Museum exhibits have a special emotional value and great power of conviction. They don't merely diversify the forms of obtaining educational information, through this fact is of no little importance in itself, but also creates special conditions for the perception of this information. This seems to be one of the reasons for the unusual interest among the public and for the steady growth of their attendance that has virtually become an explosion in the last few years.

Another objective prerequisite for the active influence of museums on universal education is their diversity, their direct connection with many sciences, branches of production and fields of culture. Museums have yet to contribute to the process of education. The study of visitors to discover what new knowledge they have gained through museums may not measure up to modern scientific requirements nor, it may allow an integrated theory of education to be developed.

Science Centres and Museums in Developing Strategies

In order to enhance the role of Science Centres and Museums in developing Strategies, we have identified several significant criteria as follows:

Exhibits: we agreed that the exhibit philosophy would be directed strongly to enhance the role of involving the visitor. The exhibit must attract the visitor, and then must challenge him, either intellectually, or physically, and to transmit the message it is intended to convey. It must inspire him with the joy of seeking knowledge, and should kindle in him a desire to know more about the subject.

The idea or application to be conveyed is first decided and thought out carefully. Then the means of conveying it are worked out. Some things, combustibles, cryogenic materials, high voltage electricity, etc., are too dangerous to be handled by inexperienced people and can only be used in a demonstration by trained demonstrators. Several of these are conducted every day, preceded of course, by announcements on the public address system.

Some more complex ideas such as orders of magnitude, urban planning, animal behaviour or automation require a sequential learning process beginning with first principals and expanding on these ideas. Frequently this can best be done by an audio - visual demonstration using lights, slides, motion pictures and artifacts or combination of any of these.

Many consider that the best exhibit category, is the visitor-operated unit which requires input from the visitor for its function, and in the process, lets the visitor learn through his own experience. For example, there is an exhibit that permits the visitor to watch the pupil of his own eye narrowing in response to increased intensity of light, or enable him to see, with one eye, the retina of the other. An example in Washington Museum that explains catching criminals using DNA fingerprinting and a transparent cow producing methane gas. These examples beautifully illustrate how new a science museum can involve its visitors in learning process. The mission of the Marion Koshland Science Museum, which recently opened in Washington, DC, is to present the facts to us and let us reach our conclusions. Associated with the National Academy of Sciences, the museum's exhibits are based on Research and Reports from the Academy that are based on the cutting edge science. Hands-on activities catch the visitors' attention and draw them in to the experience." The Wonders of Science," a permanent exhibit, tackles the question of the nature of the universe with a film about dark energy and dark matter, entities that have only recently been accepted as real. "Putting DNA to Work" discusses controversial issues in genetics, such as genetically modified foods and gene therapy for treating inherited disease. "Global Warming Facts and Our Future" explores the consequences of the green house effect and offers the viewer virtual options with which they can experiment to find solutions.

The Children's Discovery Museum

Children's Discovery Museum offers a vibrant and interactive exhibits for children from two to twelve years of age to explore, and engage senses in joyful learning. The museum gives all children the opportunity to realize their potential by providing to learn in their own way, at their own pace, through developmentally appropriate experience. Exhibits are designed to be touched, prodded, poked, tried on, and thoroughly explorer. The Museum helps children come to understand and enjoy the world in which they create.

Children's museum must be hosts a wide variety of activities and sensory experiences designed with the young child in mind. There are three types of activities you and your young child may engage in while at the Museum - active, exploratory and quiet.

We have learned that children will select what best fits their current mood and then change activities when they feel satisfied and ready to move on. For some, alternating one kind of activity with another makes the Museum experience better, while for others, choosing what to do and for how long sets the tone and pace of the visit.

Active Experiences

Young children need to move - a lot, when climbing, hopping, jumping, etc., they learn many fundamental concepts: up/down, over/under, to name a few. They figure out what their bodies can do and how to maneuver through their world. By actively exploring objects, manipulating them with their hands and twirling, pounding and turning, children experiment with concepts like weight and volume, shape, height, number and colour. They also gain much needed fine motor skills and the ability to track objects visually and coordinate eye and hand movements. The following exhibits are great for active play:

Gross Motor Skills: Pirate Ship and Lighthouse, Dance Studio, Sand Castle

Fine Motor Skills: Computers, Electric Train, Face painting, Art & Craft and Music.

Exploratory Experiences: Children are natural explorers. Instinctively, they touch, taste, hear and look at whatever is around them. Developing the ability to recognize the similarities and differences in sensory information enables them to begin associating particular sensory characteristics with certain things. Ultimately, this understanding adds order and meaning to many of their experiences. Through fantasy play, children actively explore the different qualities of people in their lives. By role - playing fire-fighter or a dancer, the child stretches his or her imagination to gain familiarity with the larger world. The following exhibits are of great for exploratory experiences: Sensory Experiences: Science room, music room, Arts & Crafts Fantasy Play: Theater, Dance Studio, and Pirate Ship.

Quite Activities: When children need a break from new and stimulating activities, they often seek familiar, repetitive activities. Reading stories in the reading corner, watching the fish in the aquarium or just sitting under the Pirate Ship are all quiet activities.

Partnerships between Museums and Schools

One key role of museums has been to partner with schools. However, in order to do so effectively, it is essential to more deeply examine and refine best practices for these partnerships. What are the mutual benefits of such collaborations? How can museums and schools more effectively partner to support learning?

Museums and schools typically have different biases, perspectives, goals, and even organizational structures.

Museum professionals need to explore strategies, models, and structures that can facilitate more meaningful relationships between schools and museum, in which:

- There would be an understanding and appreciation of the museum as a learning environment with multiple outcomes
- The concept of "learning" would be shared across both environments
- There would be an awareness that museums can be used in multiple ways, beyond conventional formats or models, such as field trips or teacher professional development
- The experiences that result from the collaboration between museums and schools would be negotiated among all parties – teacher, students, parents, and museums educators.
- The museum would be viewed not only as learning environment, but as an organization that supports, facilitates, and enhances particular kinds of learning
- Students would see the museums as a unique learning environment, supporting lifelong learning

In order for museums and schools to develop more meaningful relationships in support of earning we have identified several significant directions the field should take to improve practice and research, as follows:

- Improvement in practice will require a continued development of shared goals between museums and schools.
- Despite the constraints of standards and accountability, schools and museums share a mutual goal of creating experiences that encourage students to be critical thinkers.
- Museums should be encouraged to work collectively with local schools, as a unified voice will have the most effective impact.
- Museums should be partners with local universities where teacher education takes place.

Best example is found in Discovery Museum in London represents in a Museum Classroom as such, a school and museum space designed for and dedicated to interactive teaching and learning. This indoor or outdoor space is devoted to exploration and discovery through interaction with (but not limited to) works of art, science, mathematics, and human perception. It allows students and teachers to learn through exploration, play and experimentation with tools, materials, and other educational resources. Setting the tone for **Inspiration, Ideas, Experimentation, and Inquiry:**

Physical Components:

The environment will be organized in station for interactive learning, through explorations, investigations and pursuits of ideas. It will reflect an ever - changing.

Critique Wall

Our "middle gray" wall includes three large bulletin boards with spotlights for group and individual critiques of ongoing and completed works. Students observe, analyze and discuss their work using design elements and principles as the foundation. Students learn with classmates and the instructor during the process and return to their work with different viewpoints.

Tools and Materials Workshop Space

Areas are organized for student independent use, including art, science and technology based tools.

An in-class library

An in-class library is organized to offer books, posters and objects for Nature studies including both Storage and Display area. There is a need to establish current effective computer and audio-visual offering in the classroom both for group demonstrations and appropriate research.

Creating Artifacts

Students have created painted murals, ceramic tiles murals, and stained glass murals. Students have repaired and created art stools.

Featured Artist Space

Throughout the year, student, community, and professional artists' works are displayed. These works enhance and support curriculum. Students gain experience in displaying artwork as well as seeing a diverse body of artists work. This provides an area that highlights exemplary work as students explore mediums.

Teacher as Artist in Residence–Altered books, Light/dark ox-plow books, Sketch–book journal/sketchbook, critique session participant

Outdoor Classroom

An accessible outdoor space to the indoor classroom is developed to extend educational opportunities. This area is used for art and science investigations along with painting and drawing. It includes plants, renewable energy, and ecology, and studies of birds and insects. It also will include an amphitheatre for the Theatre Arts and Music programs. Water and electricity are included.

Service Learning

Two initiatives: Developing an Outdoor Arts/Science area adjoining the classroom and providing art activities for senior citizens at Assisted Living Residence.

Cooperative Learning

Students will teach one another and will serve as positive role models for younger students. They may become Explorers who also conduct workshops for other classes or schools.

Technology

Websites, group emails, In focus / computer set up/ projection area.

Electronic Handouts and on-line learning, Digital camera, Slide projector, overhead, opaque

Other good stuff

Magnetic tape, Idea pole, Retractable laundry line Paint palettes with clear plastic covers, Chromacryl paints, engraver

Mobile Science Museums

Villages account for nearly 75% of the total population in our country. To meet their needs, to make them conscious of science and technology and of their duty towards mankind, to the environment, the land, health, family institutions, society, education, employment - all influenced by science and technology - special methods are required. The city dweller does not feel lost among the many changes taking place about him: he is directly or indirectly involved. Moreover, various agencies are engaged in brining new knowledge and understanding to city dwellers.

The picture is completely different in the villages. There, people are shielded from all these influences, and their prevailing attitude towards their environment is non-scientific.

They are never brought to imagine that a scientific temperament is essential to them. Nor do schools deal with this problem, nor is there any agency seriously interested in wiping out the ignorance of villagers. Dynamic science education, in a proper perspective, may be the only solution. Quick, interesting new method can solve the difficulty.

Science Centres and Museums should realize this long - standing need and may develope science exhibitions on mobile units (car and trailer) which are taken to the doors of rural people. The exhibits should be simple, concise, impressive coherent and include models, instruments, dealing with different branches / disciplines of science.

Visitor studies

Science centres and museums have gained increasing importance over the last ten years. Their hands-on style makes them something between a museums and a fun fair and, beyond the issue of merit, no doubt the success of many science centres also depends on providing education through entertainment.

It is important then to be able to assess to what extent people can actually make use of the proposed theme. Science centres and museums must act as an interface for dialogue with the people. A research of this kind should not limit itself to museums, because public opinion on scientific subjects is also influenced by more popular and widespread media such as newspapers and television. Together with people, museums should therefore also be able to make good use of these media and offer opportunities for investigating and going into detail about given topics that the other media deal with without leaving enough time for thinking them over.

Workshops

Science centres and museums should encourage workshops on a variety of subjects as described below.

Playing with light

We've done several variations on this workshop, but here is how we described one them at the Science Museum:

Goals of the Workshop

- Experiment with lights and variety of crafts materials to see what the possibilities are.
- Learn how you can use programming to make even a single light do many things.
- Design and program something interesting that incorporates sensors, light, and physical material.

Materials

- Computers
- Crickets
- LEDs and wires, as well as switches, sensors, and motors
- Shiny and translucent craft & recycled materials: straws, plastic portion (or nut) Cups, reflective contact paper, tinsel, glitter, beads, etc.
- Low-temperature hot melt glue

Learning languages

Most developed country has second language English therefore science centres and museums should be learning English courses for learning from books, literatures, all the world websites and other media.

Computer and Internet

Science centres and museums should be training students' classes on computer. These classes may be designed to appeal to all of learning modes with a carefully woven fabric of lecture, hands-on, and interaction. Scientific museums should be encouraged to use computer in life.

Science centres and museums should be encouraged to use internet. Museum websites may have begun as digital brochures and developed subsequently into online representations of the physical museum, but they have not stopped there. Generally resisting the temptation to use the latest special effects for their own sake, they show considerable diversity of content, design, philosophy and navigational practice; and offer effective learning experience on the internet. While not professing to play the same kind of role as commercially produced games, many museum websites provide enjoyable and meaningful experiences in which the representation of objects and artifacts and the motivation and active engagement of learners are clearly paramount.

Environment

Science centres and Museum display and activities are imaginatively designed, to enhance understanding of man's physical being and the interaction between man and his environment. The exhibitions may include fascinating, interactive, hands-on displays dealing with anatomy, physiology and health education.

Science centres and Museum also should be encouraged to learn environment, how to keep environment clean from pollutions (water, air and earth).

Scientific Trips

Museums should be encouraged scientific trips to desert to study the sedimentary, igneous, metamorphic rocks, plants, structures of the rocks, animals and visit beaches of the sea to study waves of the water, types of fishes, plants sea water and planktonic also visit rivers to study plants, animals of brackish water to learn about scientific environments in nature.

Laboratories

Laboratories where activities and experiments take place in many scientific subjects such as: chemistry, physics, optics, electricity, physiology etc.

Lectures

Museums should be encouraged to organize scientific lectures to learn and discuss topics related to different branches of science.

Libraries

Museums should be encouraged to read simple scientific books.

Conclusions

From the above mentioned, we can conclude that the enhanced role of science centres and museums would involve good connections between museums and schools, beautiful, entertaining, and simple exhibits, use of computers and internet, simple experiments, simple lectures and books, study nature environments, Hands-on exhibits, simple workshops for children's and spread scientific cultural in villages.

- The role of discovery museums is important in imparting scientific knowledge to the people.
- Connection between museums and schools must be maintained.

- Mobile museums have an important role to play in the rural areas.
- Opinions of visitors helps improve strategies and methodologies.
- Environment education needs to be emphasized.
- The role of training computers and internet cannot be undermined.
- Children should be at the centre-stage.

Acknowledgements

The author feels greatly indebted to Prof. Dr. Fawzi A Elrefaie, President and Prof. Dr. Mohsen M. Shoukry, Vice-President of the Academy of Scientific Research and Technology for nominating me to participate in the African Regional Conference on the Enhanced Role of Science Centres and Museums in the Development Strategies, Lusaka, Zambia, 10-14 January 2006.

References

- Chakraborti, R. M. 1774. Museum of exact and natural sciences. V.XXVI. No. 2.1974 pp.118-121
- Anderson, D. *et al.*, 2005. Partnership between Museums and Schools. pp. 38-40 PrincipleinPractice@ilinet.org
- Il Museiums. 2004. National Museum of Science, Technology and Space http: // www.ilmuseums.comm/ museum-eng.asp?id=6
- Deen, B.B. 2003. Review on Explore & Discover. London http: // word .std.com/ ~ brd/museum classroom.htm
- Hawkey, R. 2004. Learning with digital Technologies in Museums, Science and Galleries home http:// www.nestafuturelab.org/research/reviews/o9 21.htm
- Schultz, P.2004 Science Friday Kids' Connection – in association with Kidsnet, April 23, 2004, Hour Tow: Science Museums http:// www.sciencefriday com/Kids/ sfke20040423-2html

- Crespi, M. 2001, Museums and Museums: the picture of scientific museums http://jeklyll.comm.sissa.it/articoli/art05_05_02_eng.htm
- Science Museum of Minnesota. 2005. SMM Computer Education Centre: Why the Education Centre? http://composed.smm.org/about/why.htm
- PIE. Playfully Inventing & Exploring with Digital & other Stuff, 2005. Workshops http://www.pienetwork.org/work.org/workshops.

Five Decades of Science Museum Movement in India

Tapan K Ganguly
Director, Science City, Kolkata, India
E-mail: sctycal@cal.vsnl.net.in

We are meeting at a difficult cross road of history when the human civilization is tormented by divisive forces bringing in insurmountable barriers of language, region and ethnicity. The need for national integration and international fraternity is very seriously felt today when this beautiful world of ours stands like a house divided. Efforts to save the world from possible disaster cannot be the task of handful of institutions like the United Nations or the Red Cross or organisations like NAM S&T Centre or a few individuals. It is the people at large who have to be motivated to develop the right attitude towards making this wonderful world congenial for living. Museum, which is recognised as a very effective platform for non-formal education, can play a vital role at this crucial moment in rendering service to the mankind by reorganising its activities and rescheduling its priorities in order to achieve the goal of global integration. Through interactive and innovative presentation of artifacts and activities the museums are in a position to motivate the people to shed their differences and unite for the survival of mankind. Science centers and museums can play a pivotal role in achieving this objective.

Museums discover the past to better understand the present for appropriately planning the future. They collect and preserve the evidences of natural and physical worlds and human achievements and use these collections and associated ideas to add to human knowledge and understanding. Till the middle of 20th century museums were considered as grimfaced storehouses of artifacts with mostly passive display. The museums on the whole were apparently meant for only intellectuals and scholars and common people preferred to stay away from them. However, upon realising that the museums could be utilised as useful and effective tools in achieving social transformation, the approaches of the museum managers have undergone a change for betterment during the past few decades. The museums are now becoming dynamic institutions and more people oriented as opposed to the earlier concept of being object oriented. However, this welcome change in paradigm of the museums did not occur in isolation by virtue of the wisdom of few intellectuals and foresighted museum managers. It is the demand of the society which made this change possible. The museums gradually broke away from the old conventional concept of touch-me-not exhibits. The science museums and centres went a step further by introducing hands-on, interactive presentations which transformed them into vibrant dynamic institutions upholding the famous Chinese saying:

> I read, I forget,
> I see, I remember,
> I do, I understand.

India was one of the pioneers among the developing countries in realising the importance of science museums in popularising science among the common people. After independence in 1947, India witnessed a great surge of interest in science, technology and industry. During the 1950s scientific research was given a tremendous boost and to meet the growing need of trained technical manpower in the country, great emphasis was given to establish science and technological institutions. There was a growing realisation that science had to be propagated and popularised amongst the masses, so as to improve the quality of life for the people and to make the common man aware of the power that science can wield in overall national development. Science museums were a natural corollary of all these.

The science museum movement in India started with the setting up of an industrial museum in 1954 on the campus of the Birla Institute of Technology and Science in Pilani, about 200 kilometres south-west of Delhi. This was followed by a nucleus science museum set up in the National Physical Laboratory (NPL) in New Delhi in 1957. While the Central Museum in Pilani remained confined to its limited audience, the nucleus science museum in NPL became an instant hit with the visitors who were primarily students and people from the scientific community. Unfortunately, the novel experiment of NPL had to be abruptly closed due to the heavy rush of visitors to the museum which impeded the research work at the Laboratory.

The first science museum to cater to the country's general public opened its doors in Kolkata on May 2, 1959. The Birla Industrial and Technological Museum was set up under the auspices of the Council of Scientific & Industrial Research, Government of India. The exhibits of the museum were generally built with a strong pedagogic approach. Armed with the experience gained and the in-house infrastructural facilities developed, the Museum in Kolkata undertook the task of setting up the country's second science museum in Bangalore, some 2000 kilometres south-west of Kolkata, which was opened in 1965. It was only after 12 years that the third such institution came into being in Mumbai; but this time it was a science centre.

Museum movement in India got a fillip at the hands of the national leaders and due importance was assigned on systematic development of science museums. The Planning Commission of the Government of India realised the great potential of the science museums in the community development and a Task Force was set up which stipulated the guidelines, area and scope of activities of the science museums of the country. The Task Force in their recommendation (1974) urged for the establishment of a central coordinating agency to pool and optimise the available resources, to carry out free exchange of exhibits and personnel between museums under its control, to promote research and training facilities for sustained growth of activities and the development of new science centres in the country. The Task Force suggested a four tier decentralized system in order to reach the people at large. First of all four major science museums or centres of national status were to be developed in four zones of the country to support a chain of regional and district/sub-regional science centres having primary objective of conducting outreach activities in their respective regions. At the grass root level Mobile Science Exhibition units, controlled from the local science centres were to travel through the interior of the country.

The Task Force recommendation boosted the science museum movement of the country beyond expectations. The National Council of Science Museums (NCSM) was set up in 1978 as the central coordinating agency to ensure coordination and support. The authorities of NCSM decided to implement the Task Force report in a phased manner and India witnessed a spurt of activities in the field of science centre development. Four national level science museums and centres started functioning from Kolkata, Bangalore, Mumbai and Delhi. Nine regional science centres were set up at the state capitals or major cities and several district/sub-regional science centres were established at district headquarters or small towns spread across the country. In addition a fleet of Mobile Science Exhibition units was introduced to crisscross the country through out the year. A Central Research & Training

Laboratory had also been built for proper development of exhibits and manpower resources. From three units in 1978, the NCSM network grew to 14 units in 1993 and 28 in 2003 and a total of 35 centres were developed up to 2005. Other functional major science centres outside NCSM umbrella are located at Pilani, Chennai, Hyderabad, Jaipur, Trivandrum and Agartala. These centres and the NCSM units are in continuous dialogue on various issues related to science communication.

Presentation by the museums and centres of NCSM are multi-disciplinary in nature - both in form and in themes. In addition to permanent thematic exhibitions in galleries there are open-air science parks and mobile science exhibition units. Year round activities for students include programmes such as science seminar (elocution contest), science quiz, science fair, hobby centre, nature study camp, telescope making and sky observation and some others. Special programmes for older people such as teachers' training programme, vocational training programme, seminars and training workshop are also held regularly. Popular demonstration lectures, science dramas, science marches and temporally exhibitions are some of the other programmes organized regularly for general visitors. Varied subjects are covered through exhibits and activities. Although there are certain features in common in terms of the content, the science museums and centres under NCSM carefully avoid regimentation in concept and approach. While the major museums and centres at the 4 metros deal with the exhibits having national and international context, the character and format of regional and district/sub-regional science centres vary from one another even though certain core exhibits and activities on basic sciences are common to all of them. In effect utility based activities and supporting exhibits are typical of each centre. Because of the vast territory and the diversity in social and cultural patterns requirements and relevance are different in different places. Regional and district/sub-regional science centres are therefore oriented more towards specific local needs and problems.

The Industrial & Technological Museums in Kolkata and Bangalore went through radical changes during 1965-70 when they provided the necessary infrastructure for launching a massive outreach programme through mobile science exhibitions, science demonstration lectures, teachers' training programmes, creative ability centres and other educational programmes. With the advent of the Science Centre in Mumbai in 1977 the Museums were gradually transformed into dynamic institutions, vibrant with activities. More and more people were attracted to their non-formal teaching and learning processes through interactive exhibits and hands-on activities. The trend continued for nearly quarter of a century during which period new science centres sprung up almost at all parts of the country. The interactive exhibits of the newer science centres not only kindled imagination but also made science easier to understand by the common people. All these activities meant sustained demand for a large number of exhibits mostly of working and interactive types, a variety of science kits and also demonstration aids.

The educational programmes and other activities of the Indian science museums and centres are generally focused towards definite target groups. This approach has undoubtedly made them buzzing hives of activity involving people from various age groups, of which the students have become the main beneficiaries. This has formed a notion in some minds that the science centres are only for students and children. To dispel this misconception the science centres in India are constantly devising newer and novel approaches to suit the tastes of a wide cross-section of people. The most remarkable achievement in this direction is the establishment of Science City in Kolkata in the summer of 1997 which is essentially a science centre, but with a difference. The exhibits here are not only interactive but also experience based, not only hands-on but also minds-on. The grand success of this NCSM centre has prompted others to follow suit and two more science cities had been set up, one at the north at Jullandhar (Punjab) and the other at the west at Gandhinagar (Gujarat) by the respective State Governments. A Regional Science City is also being developed at Lucknow by NCSM which will open its doors within a few months.

Infrastructure development had been the top priority of NCSM from the beginning. During the past years a wide network covering almost the entire country had been established. This growth in physical establishments - buildings, facilities, equipments, trained manpower etc. has put the council on a solid base. Starting from the science centre at Mumbai, design and construction of all new science centres of NCSM were done departmentally. Landscape design and development of the campus including the science parks were also done by the Council staff. All NCSM units have well developed exhibit making workshops which are fully capable of developing exhibits not only for them but also for others. This exhibit development expertise of NCSM units is now recognised internationally. This is reflected in a continuous demand for catalytic support from other science centres and similar institutions in India and abroad. In the recent past NCSM has given exhibits to science centres in Australia, U. K., Israel, Turkey and Bangladesh. The first Science Centre in Mauritius has been set up by NCSM on a turnkey basis. Several other proposals for setting up new science centres in other countries are also being received by the National Council of Science Museums.

In the recent past India had witnessed a significant growth in science popularisation activities. A number of science centres are being developed by the central and some state governments. A few industrial houses are contemplating to set up special S & T expositions to showcase their own activities and products. The NCSM is in great demand by all of them to conceive and develop those new centres. This unprecedented growth of science popularisation activities has led to the shortage of qualified and trained manpower in the relevant field. In order to bridge the gap between demand and supply NCSM had recently introduced a Master of Science course in Science Communication in association with one of the premiere S & T institutions of India. The Faculty for the course is drawn from the most renowned Universities and Engineering Institutes of India. The Smithsonian institution, Washington D.C. provides visiting faculty members for some selected topics. The first batch of students has been inducted in 2005 and there shall be fresh intake in July 2006. The eligibility of the candidates for the course is either Bachelor of Engineering or Master of Science degree in selected disciplines and sponsored candidates shall be given preference. The course is also open for overseas candidates.

The science museums and science centres of India have evolved considerably during the last five decades and are still in constant pursuit of excellence. Multifarious programmes are continuously being devised to meet the diverse requirements and expectations of the target groups. It is this approach which is bringing them far closer to the community than ever before resulting in increased visitor inflow to them. To keep the visitors coming to the museums again and yet again the science centres of NCSM are constantly creating brilliant exhibits and generating newer and more novel activities to supplement the exhibits on display. They have also geared up to share their expertise with other similar or like minded institutions.

The Enhanced Role of Science Centres and Museums in Development Strategies

Abhay Kothari
Director
Manthan Educational Programme Society,
C-1, Sukruti, Manekbaug, Ahmedabad-380 015. (India)
Email : Manthan@satyam.net.in

In the present age where technology rules almost every action undertaken by us, knowledge of Science and Technology, and a vibrant populace are assets that the developing countries must focus on. For this purpose, the role of Science Centres and Museums becomes crucial. Not only for scientific development, but for general benefits also, techniques of science are useful. A simple example could be that of building a solar powered generator in a village for rural electrification, or at a more complex level, developing satellites for the purpose of education. Thus, we see how crucial it is to spread scientific awareness.

In this article, we would focus on the role of Science Centres and Museums in development strategies. As a matter of fact; the numbers of science centre and science museums, which have been built in India, an upcoming developing country, serve hardly 0.0001 per cent of the population. This means that the majority of the population does not have access to science education through science museums or Science Centres. If we are to assess the consequences of this, we need to find out the relevance of these centres of scientific education. Science centres & Museums have a great role to play in designing developmental strategies to communicate Science to people. We live in a world dominated by Science & Technology and to be ignorant of science is to be ignorant of life around us.

An important step in the direction of enhancing the role of museums and science centres could be after a natural calamity, or much better before something of the sort occurs, to make people aware of the science behind it, so that people do not link it to superstition.

In India, we find a dichotomy, where on one hand; there is widespread technological awareness in IT hubs like Hyderabad and Bangalore, and on the other, there are beliefs among people that natural calamities occur because of some wrong-doings of theirs in the past life. This is what finds employment for godmen and others of the kind.

India is vulnerable to natural disasters like Tsunami, Bird flu, Earthquake, and also manmade disasters (like the Bhopal gas tragedy) and hence there is need for greater scientific awareness and understanding among the masses. This calls for the development of participatory exhibits and low cost materials to explain and face up to such phenomena in an appropriate manner. Manthan has organized short term programmes on these topics which were very effective by using this material.

For example, after the earthquake in Kutch in 2001, the kits developed by Vigyan Prasar and designed by us on 'Understanding Earthquakes' became very popular amongst students and the community. This served a dual purpose, firstly, there was better understanding of the earthquake related phenomena along scientific lines, and secondly and more importantly, there was spread of scientific awareness and its importance among the youngsters. It may be noted that Manthan used low cost toys and other material to explain matters like precautions to be taken before, during and after an earthquake. As an example, a simple slinky was used to explain seismic waves.

We concluded from the above exercise that existing exhibits and programmes could be made very effective by using participatory elements in the exhibits. That is because putting an idea in the form of an interactive exhibit is very different from an explanation or experiment in the laboratory. Our exhibition on Solar Eclipse helped communities understand this phenomenon. It also helped generate awareness against superstitions associated with eclipses. Over a million people used the safe solar viewer to view the eclipse in 1999. Our experience taught us that getting the community to be a part of the experiment helps generate and maintain interest in the activities. Manthan has designed several activity kits related to scientific phenomena in order to get the children involved. Once interest is generated and curiosity aroused, the students continue to be interested in the subject. The activity kits consist of components like colouring pictures, making cutouts and, simple information booklets, do-it-yourself experiments and many such related activities.

Low cost thematic science kits and other carry home materials generate great interest. A child or a member of the community takes away a mini museum idea to his/her home. It is in effect a mobile science centre! Manthan also designed some Interactive Radio Programmes outreach material for National Council for

Science & Technology Communication / DST, Government of India. Manthan distributed the kits to registered listeners, which could be used according to the instructions on the radio. This was a very popular show and generated a lot of response and enthusiasm from students.

Before the Radio programme on Biodiversity, we sent thematic science toys made from paper to the registered listeners. Our kit on Nature designed for the 'National Natural History Museum', New Delhi, was very popular amongst students. The material was designed in such a way that by displaying, one could set up a mini museum on his/her table.

Jathas have been another innovative way employed by Manthan as Low cost travelling exhibition. They act as mobile science centres, and feasible for developing countries. Two reasons can be pointed out for this. Firstly, because they are low cost in assembling, and secondly, because they are made from locally available resources. This makes them more easy-to-identify-with in a rural set-up. In the North-Western parts on India, camels and bullock carts are widely used as modes of transportation. Manthan made use of this to take science to rural areas.

Our Camel Cart Science Expo went from village to village with science exhibition, participatory toys, mini library and puppet show. These were items that the villagers were familiar with and at the same time were interested in, so it was easier to get them to participate in the activities, than through a typical museum or science centre where things are displayed with captions, but which a rural person finds difficult to operate.

It was cost effective, local, and excitable and communicated through the vernacular medium. It is a classic example of where the villagers can not come to the prestigious science centres, but the centres go to them.

Another aspect of science popularization that must go hand in hand to make the science centres more effective is the building up of local and regional networks with common objectives that can help in dissemination of developmental ideas faster. These networks can help communicate common contents, information, ideas, and objectives. This also makes it easy to implement common programmes. This can be facilitated by having a network of Non-Government Organisations working at grass root levels. Another way is to take the district level administration into confidence which can lead to smooth functioning of any science popularisation related projects.

Our local network in Kutch is working with Regional and international networks in the field of Science and Technology entrepreneurship programme of Anjar Knife manufacturers. This district of Gujarat is famous for its knives, but there were a number of problems. One was the lack of innovation in the design of the knives which proved to be a hindrance in the sense that the obsolete designs were not very populars in the market. Also, the knives were made in the little village of Nanareha and were sold at lower rates to middlemen who made huge profits. So, the original craftsperson was not getting the required level of profit. In collaboration with the National Institute of Design, Ahmedabad, new designs were created for these knife manufactures. A German exchange student worked on this project and also paid a visit to Anjar to get an idea of the ground reality.

Manthan participated in a big way in the Jathas also, the mobile exhibition with eye catching posters and games and promoted scientific thinking.

Conclusion

Museum and Science centres provide an excellent media to communicate science for developmental causes. The only area where action needs to be taken is in making them reach out to larger strata of the society and get more people oriented towards it. There is a lot that can be done other than governmental measures. NGOs can play an important role and substantiate the governmental measures with those of their own.

It is imparative to remember that "What needs to be communicated?" is clear and well defined.

Developmental programmes can be made effective by creating participatory and thematic exhibition. Museums can reach larger segment of the society through that innovative outreach programmes. Developmental ideas can be disseminated through local traveling exhibits, low cost material and folk performances with the help of networks, which can disseminate developmental ideas among the masses. Workshops can be conducted, and travelling museums can percolate into remote areas. From exhibitions on camels in Northern India to Science teachers travelling on elephant backs to reach villages not connected by roads, science communication should be open to new approaches.

Finally, it is important that the process of science communication does not stop at the level of dissemination of information. To be more effective, it is important that this knowledge is used for implementation of developmental programmes. Schemes need to be initiated for this purpose.

Role of Science Centres and Museums in Pakistan

Alia Bano Munshi
Principal Scientific Officer
PCSIR Labs. Complex, Karachi (Pakistan)
E-mail: munshi5@cyber.net.pk

Abstract

Pakistan is a developing country where problems are the same as in other developing countries. Our new generation is very good in science subjects and would like to become doctors or engineers and even take on economics or commerces - thanks to pressure from the parents. But, very few would like to study history as a subject. In Pakistan, to visit a museum has a different sense. University , college, and school students do visit museums to gain knowledge about past and take interest in ancient civilizations considering it as a treasure of our nation. The gap between Science and History is the reason there is no link between science centres and museums in Pakistan. There is need to create a basic relationship between science centres and museums in Pakistan. We are in need to do so and with passage of time, it may become compulsory in our educational system.

Key words: Pakistan, museum, science and science centres, recent situation, development strategies.

Introduction

The Islamic Republic of Pakistan emerged on the map of the world as an independent sovereign state on 14th August 1947, as a result of the division of the former British India.

Located in South Asia, Pakistan shares an eastern border with India and a north-eastern border with China. Iran makes up the country's south-west border, and Afghanistan runs along its western and northern edge. The Arabian Sea is Pakistan's southern boundary with 1,064 km of coastline.

The country has a total area of 796,095 sq km and is nearly four times the size of the United Kingdom. From Gwadar Bay in its south-eastern corner, the country extends more than 1,800 km to the Khunjerab Pass on China's border.

The museums in Pakistan house, among other things, a variety of old paintings, including some by great masters, original manuscripts in different languages and artifacts from South East Asia and the Indo-Pak sub-continent. In Pakistan there is a sizeable a number of museums as listed below.

- **Bahawalpur Museum**

The Punjab government has invested a sum of Rs. 30 million on the development of Bahawalpur museum. Museum director Hafiz Husain Ahmed Madni has announced six new galleries for the preservation of artifacts. Several antiques have been added, raising the total number of galleries to 11. Two new halls for visitors have been constructed for the display of antiques, including those from Cholistan. There is a proposal to construct a model Cholistan village at a cost of Rs10 million where antiques of Cholistan desert will be displayed to attract visitors."

Other Museums:

- Archaeological Museum, Bhambhore, Thatta.
- Bhit Shah, Hyderabad, Sind.
- (The Bhitshah Cultural Centre includes a museum and cultural centre)

- Agricultural Museum, Faisalabad
- Harappa Archaeological Museum
- Fort Museum, Pucca Fort, Hyderabad
- Sind Provincial Museum, Hyderabad
- Lok Virsa National Museum of Folk and Traditional Heritage, Islamabad
- National Museum, Islamabad
- National Museum of Pakistan, Karachi
- National History Museum, Karachi
- Quaid-i-Azam Birthplace Museum, Karachi
- Allama Iqbal Museum, Lahore
- Lahore Fort Museum, Lahore
- Central Museum, Lahore
- Faqir Khana Museum, Lahore
- Holy Museum of the Badshahi Masjid, Lahore
- Museum of Science and Technology, Lahore
- Zoological Museum, Lahore
- Guide's Mess, Museum and Cemetery, Mardan
- Mohenjodaro Archaeological Museum, Mohenjodaro
- Museum á Rawalpindi, Army Museum, Peshawar
- Saidu Sharif Archaeological Museum
- Library and Museum at Birthplace of Allama Iqbal, Sialkot
- Archaeological Museum, Taxila
- Archaeological Museum, Umarkot

On independence, Pakistan inherited seven museums. Museums at Lahore and Peshawar were run by the Provincial Governments, while site museum at Harappa, Mohenjodaro,

Taxila, and the Armoury Museum in Lahore Fort were looked after by the Central Government through its Department of Archaeology.

Immediately after independence plans were taken in hand to establish National Museum of Pakistan. It was on 17th April 1950 that the National Museum of Pakistan was inaugurated in Freer Hall building, replacing the defunct Victoria Museum.

In order to advise the National Museum of Pakistan to enrich its collection through new acquisitions, an Advisory Council for the purchase of antiquities and works of Arts was established by the government in 1950.

The development of museums in the country has been spectacular and the last few decades have seen quite a few museums being established and many others reorganized on modern lines. Recently, a museum exclusively devoted to Allama Iqbal at Javed Manzil, Lahore, and another, House Museum in the Quaid-I-Azam House (Flag Staff House), Karachi have been established.

National Museum of Pakistan at Karachi was established in 1949. It is a journey through the History of Ancient Civilizations covering archaeology, history, ancient manuscripts, historical records, numismatics and ethnology.

On the far side of Zamzama in Lahore is the Central Museum built in Mughal Gothic style and opened in 1894. It is one of the best museums in Pakistan with superb collection of relics from the rich cultural heritage of Lahore. The rare collection of Mughal paintings, statues of Buddha in various attitudes including the priceless 'Fasting Buddha'. On display are various examples of Gandhara sculpture reflecting the successive stages of the oriental civilization, miniature paintings, and manuscripts.

  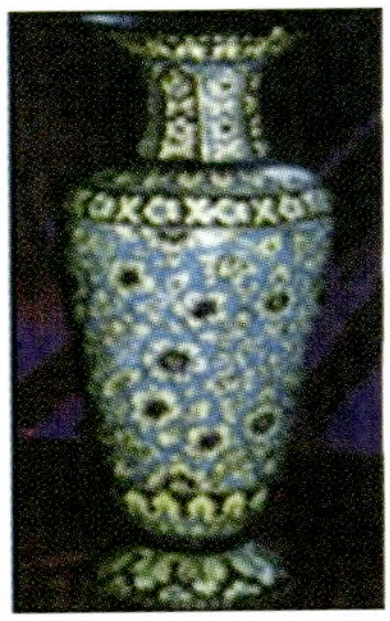

At the entrance of the gallery, large relief map of vast territory of South-Western Asia shows routes that linked various regions. Inside the gallery is chronologically placed material from Stone Age, village cultures of Baluchistan and the great Indus Valley Civilization, which flourished more than a millennium from 2500 BC, influencing an area four times that of ancient Sumer. Harappa and Mohenjodaro are now known as twin capital of this vast urban civilization.

What surprises the modern mind is careful town planning that went into building up Mohenjodaro. The carefully laid-out streets, well-aligned houses, the efficient water-supply and drainage system and rectangular blocks pre-suppose the rule of well-established and strong civil authority enforcing strict laws. Numismatics Section of National Museum stores a large number of coins from the earliest punch marked pieces to 19th century. A few enlarged models of gold coins, among these, the one found in Banbhore, bearing the name of Abbasid Caliph, Wasiq Billah, minted in Egypt in 884 AD are also on display.

Ethnological gallery, on its western side, shows representative collection of the living culture of various tribal, semi-tribal and part of the rural population, living in different regions of Pakistan.

The mission of the Museum and Science centre is to provide experiential pathways to lifelong learning in science for children and adults through exhibits, programs, and films. However, there is no concept about bonding between museums and science centres in Pakistan. During recent years, experts in the science of learning in Pakistan have tried to determine what and how people learn through museum experiences by realizing their important role. An estimated 120 million visitors entered science centres and museums in the United States in 2000, suggesting museums play an extremely important role in informal education. However, because visits to museums serve social, entertainment, and educational purposes, and because museum visits are almost always unstructured and of very short duration, it is difficult to quantify how much museum-goers carry from their visits.

French beach, Karachi: The Clifton beach in Karachi is one of the longest city beaches in the world. Although it suffered a *Tasmen aspirit* oil spill disaster, the beach has been cleaned and has floodlights installed for night-time visitors. There are also several other excellent beaches near the city such as Sandspit,

Hawke's Bay, the French Beach, Russian beach and Paradise Point (a sandstone rock promotory with a natural arch) that are frequented by visitors. The imagery is colourful, wholesome, and teeming with people on weekends.

Science centres and museums can also help attract people from ethnic minorities into science. In all over the world, museums and science centres are increasing their educational programs for children and teachers. According to the survey, 80 per cent of Pakistanis are in favour of this activity, especially during summer vacations. Many Government organizations and NGOs have shown interest, and have sponsored teacher education workshops for those working in schools. Museums and science centres have devoted considerable resources for preparing future pre-service teachers. Over 20 per cent of survey respondents provided museum staff to teach education courses or workshops at local colleges. Twenty per cent indicated they were working with universities on education research projects; and nearly 50 per cent provided resource kits for training programs for future teachers. A handful of museums also produce instructional materials.

Although the primary focus of science and technology centres is on communicating facts and concepts, they can also put issues into a social context and thus engage the public in meaningful debate about the effects of science and technology. Many exhibitions have been designed to mirror heated conflict in the province about the use of natural resources. Museum visitors were challenged to work through competing scenarios of how logging, mining, and environmental protection could co-exist.

By engaging the public in the messy process of scientific and technological decision-making, concepts such as risk, constraints, and trade-offs no longer are of theoretical importance but also of practical value. Museums and science centres can contribute to technological literacy, particularly through exhibits that encourage hands-on, problem-solving, and engineering-design activities.

The theme of this conference - Museum for Science and Industry is "think, build, test, do it again" - encourages visitors to use the same steps engineers use to design and build boats, bridges, windmills, and airplanes and then to test their performance in water tanks, shake tables, and wind tunnels.

The role of science centres

I believe that science centers and museums have an important role to play in taking forward this agenda and engaging the public with science and the developmental issues it raises in the society. In Pakistan, less people visit museums than go to theme parks and concerts. Only a few people visit science centres and science museums each year in the countries of Asia, missing a wonderful opportunity for raising their awareness on current research, providing a neutral venue for debate and dialogue, and stimulating an interest in science among the young people.

Pakistan has to develop its science museums and their relationship with the people. The National Museums and Science Centres, should host conferences, and seminars by inviting students to develop a tradition of bringing the public together on topics related to science and technology.

Science sector in the Pakistan has grown significantly in the past 20 years, but only in Colleges and Universities.

A science museum is created by its contents and the activities relating to them. These contents may be historical artifacts, such as a steam engine, or exhibits of natural phenomena, scientific ideas or technological inventions. A museum is an educational county fair, a serious and exciting learning environment where the relationships between one exhibit and the next, and among the exhibits, the visitors and the space as a whole are important. This location-and-object specific attribute sets museums apart from other communications media such as television, books and periodicals. Science centres exhibit scientific phenomena and ideas as well as objects, machines and instruments. They show the activities of scientists, the consequences of technological advancement, and the state of our knowledge of the universe; and also ourselves. They excel at presenting examples of natural phenomena, human and animal behaviour, and real-world applications of science. They provide multiple opportunities for the people to broaden and deepen their knowledge and understanding of science, technology and the natural phenomena.

The exhibits in the science museums present natural phenomena, technological innovations and scientific ideas in ways that prompt visitors, interacting with them, to ask questions and reinforce their own learning. Exhibits are designed to isolate a piece of nature or concepts from the complex world so that a visitor has a chance to poke at, fiddle with and thereby begin to comprehend it.

Museums also can provide a vivid experience of the scientific discovery process by presenting or recreating actual events such as the reception and analysis of live images from the Pioneer and Voyager space craft as they sweep past the planets.

In our young generation, we have seen a dramatic change in the daily routines of family life. In Pakistan, millions of children between the ages of 6 and 14 live in families where both parents or the sole caregiver work outside the home. More than 75 per cent of mothers with school-age children hold paying jobs. Yet many parents cannot afford after-school programs for their kids. Between 5 million and 7 million "latchkey children" come home each afternoon to an unsupervised house or apartment, where the only activity they can pursue is watching television, playing video games, or hanging out with friends. These children are vulnerable.

All children, regardless of family structure or income level, must accomplish certain developmental tasks to mature into healthy, productive adults. Today, private- and public-sector attention is increasingly focused on providing safe, supportive places for children to spend their after-school time. This is particularly important in low-income communities, where children are less likely to have access to effective schools or organized after-school activities.

Influential philanthropic organizations have been addressing this issue, raising the level of dialogue with their research, policy briefings, publications, and funding initiatives. Almost 70-90 per cent of parents said they felt that children and teens should have some kind of organized activity or place to go after school. After-school programs keep children safe, help working families, and teach academic skills. And I am willing to support this campaign.

The challenge

The challenge we must now face together is how science centres and museums can deliver the new science and society agenda and I would like to give some examples of the innovations that are already taking place in the UK.

The Darwin Centre

The Natural History Museum is, I think, leading the world with its imaginative and innovative venture at the new Darwin Centre.

The Dana Centre

The Science Museum has taken an important initiative to engage new adult audiences in topical issues in current science and technology. This Museum is presenting a regular stream of innovative events. The centre is intended to engage young adults in the age group 18-40 years using new digital technology to ensure that these events reach a wide audience outside the centre.

BNFL visitor centre at Sellafield

For controversial issues it is all too easy for the debate to become polarised and unproductive. A recent initiative by British Nuclear Fuels Ltd at their visitor centre at Sellafield is very interesting in this context. As part of its efforts to foster a genuine public debate, BNFL invited the Science Museum to exercise complete editorial independence over an exhibition, aptly named 'sparking reaction'.

SciZmic: science discovery clubs network

A fourth interesting initiative is SciZmic – a network which links schools science clubs with science centers. The network runs events at science centres, and offers projects, activities, competitions, newsletters and a discussion forum for science clubs. In its pilot year, 450 young people came to SciZmic events at science centers, over 40 clubs have signed up, and SciZmic provided the junior judging panel for the annual Aventis science books prize

Conclusion

Thus museums and science centres are very important for developing countries because there must be awareness with our wonderful history and should link with advancement of our science development. Pakistan is just a new comer in this field, no doubt we have established museums as well science centres as well but need is to create a strong bonding between these two.

Strategies on Science Centres and Museums in South Africa

Richard Waller
Consultant,Greenhouse Management Services (PTY) LTD
Block D, Carlon Falco Office Park, 16 Southway,
Kelvin, Johannesburg (South Africa)
E-mail: rwaller@greenhouse.co.za

Government Strategy and Structures:

DST Corporate Strategy

Excerpts in this section are taken from the South African Department of Science and Technology's Corporate Strategy 2005/6 - 2008/10

Key Policy Developments

Preamble to Department of Science and Technology Corporate Strategy 2005/6 - 2008/10 - "Scientific Discoveries, the associated development of new technologies, and their infusion into markets are key long term drivers of economic development. This results in sustainable improvements in the quality of life of the beneficiaries. Innovation, technology mastery and diffusion of knowledge and new products and services represent the visible elements of this system. Public and private science and technology investment have high, demonstrable social returns.

Policies were developed in response to the following challenges:

- Large reduction in national R&D spend;
- The capability to respond to regional strategic risks;

- Need to renew our human resources for science and technology;
- Reduction of R&D in the private sector;
- Inadequate intellectual property legislation and infrastructure;
- Fragmented governance structures.

The following papers, policies and strategies define the South African Science and technology landscape:

- White Paper on Science and Technology (1996) created the policy framework, which continues to underpin and inform the strategic development of science and technology in South Africa.
- In 2002 the Cabinet accepted the National Research and Development Strategy as the basis for further development of the National System of Innovation (NSI) and to address key challenges to the NSI's robustness and effectiveness.
- Indigenous Knowledge System Policy was approved by Cabinet in 2004.
- The Strategic Management Framework for Science and Technology was approved by Cabinet in 2004.

Goals and Deliverables

Principal Goals of the Corporate Strategy:

- To ensure that the National System of Innovation addresses national growth and development goals in both the first and second economy;
- To develop and maintain a highly competent and representative cohort of scientists in South Africa;
- To ensure that South Africa has world class scientific infrastructure in place;

- To administer an optimal set of funding instruments;
- To respond creatively to global and continental challenges.

Technology Missions and Technology Transfer

Enhanced innovation requires the establishment and funding of technology missions that are critical to promote economic and social development. The missions identified are:

- Information technology;
- Biotechnology;
- Manufacturing technology;
- Technology to leverage knowledge and technology from and add value to our natural resources;
- Technology for poverty reduction.

The National Biotechnology Strategy was published and financed at seed level in 2002/3.

Human Resources

Our approach to human resource development is rooted in the need to radically increase the number of women and PDIs entering the sciences and remaining in the system, but on the other hand to maximise the pursuit of excellence in global terms. One way to achieve national excellence is to focus our basic science on areas where we are most likely to succeed, because of important natural or knowledge advantages. In South Africa these include

- Astronomy;
- Human Palaeontology;
- Indigenous Knowledge.

The key institution in the context of this strategy, promoting science is the National Research Foundation (NRF) linked to the higher education sector through the National Plan for Higher Education.

Investment

Across the world, in response to the increasing rates of knowledge production, dissemination and application, the shortening of product life cycles and the increasing competition for human resources – many countries are increasing their national investment in R&D.

- OEDC average 2.15% of GDP
- Finland and Korea spend far more;
- Expenditure in developing economies such as Chile and India is prioritised and rising;
- SA expenditure is 0.76% but 1% is targeted.

DST Structure

DST Organogram:

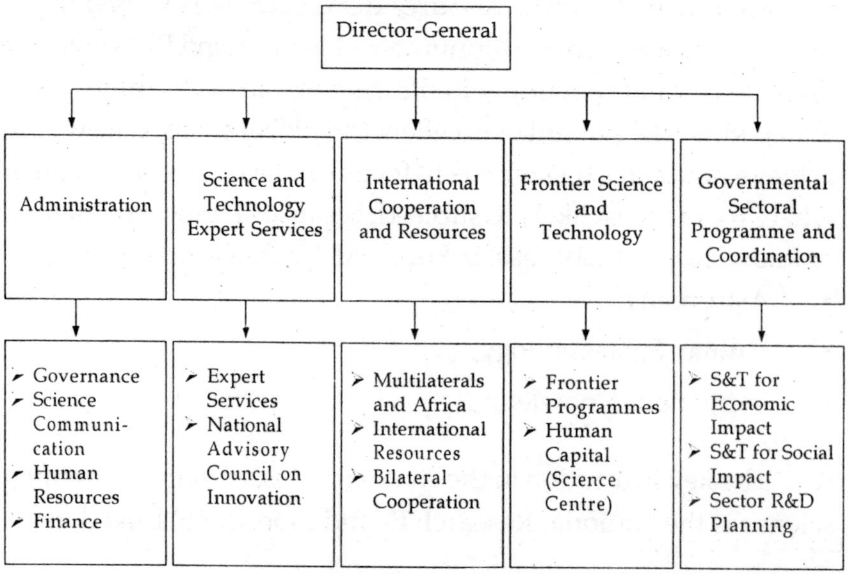

Programmes:

Programme 1: Administration

Provides support and governance functions across the Department and the broader science and technology system.

Programme 2: Science and Technology Expert Services

This programme is to support the DST by providing expert services with regard to policy, implementation, monitoring and review on science and technology initiatives.

Programme 3: International Co-operation and Resources

This programme is responsible through its three sub-programmes for the development of bilateral, polylateral, and multilateral co-operation in science and technology to strengthen the National System of Innovation, and to ensure a net flow of knowledge, capacity and resources into South Africa and the African continent.

Programme 4: Frontier Science and Technology

This programme provides leadership in respect of long-term and cross cutting research (Frontier Programmes), and human capital development. The development of a network of science centres is located here, together with the basic science areas of astronomy, human palaeontology, and indigenous knowledge systems, science communication and promotion of technological innovation. Key projects include:

- Global Earth Observation System of Systems – globally co-ordinate earth observations across a number of domains;
- Square Kilometre Array – programme to build a new world class radio telescope in South Africa and neighbouring countries;

- Open Source Software – advocating and shaping the use and application of open source software;
- South African Research Network – high speed research network interconnecting all South African research institutions, and to those located elsewhere in the world;
- Biotechnology Strategy – establishment of Regional Innovation Centres;
- Innovation Fund – securing of Intellectual Property Rights (IPR) and calls for innovation projects and funding of student innovation initiatives;
- Indigenous Knowledge Systems – set up of a Trust fund and SADC workshop to address issues of protection of indigenous knowledge;
- DST Centres of Excellence, this includes programmes in
    - Establishment of 6 Centres of Excellence;
    - Various initiatives for HR development including set up of post doctoral fellowships and professional development
    - Science and Youth, and is where the drafting of a policy for the development of a network of science centres is located;
    - National Science Week;
    - Poverty Reduction developmental initiatives within Integrated Sustainable Rural Development Strategy nodes.

Programme 5: Government Sectoral Programmes and Coordination

Provide leadership and give support to other government departments in respect of sector specific research and development and directed human capital programmes.

Other Structures

Entities and Instruments Reporting to the Minister

- Human Sciences Research Council - promotes research and knowledge in the field of human sciences;
- National Research Foundation - supports and promotes research through funding, human resource development, and the provision of resource facilities, and outreach. The South African Agency for Science and Technology Advancement (SAASTA) originally FEST now reports to the NRF, and is the agency most directly involved in Science Centre governance and development and is the project manager for the development of a network of science centres;
- Council for Scientific and Industrial Research - mandate is to foster industrial and scientific development;
- Africa Institute of South Africa - statutory body focussing on political, socio-economic, international and development issues in contemporary Africa;
- Godisa Trust - innovation and technology demonstration activities and incubator programme initiated and co-financed with the EU;
- Tshumisano Trust - operates Technology Stations Programme with funding from DST and GTZ, to strengthen and accelerate interaction between Technikons and SMMEs
- Academy of Science of South Africa - promote a common ground in scientific thinking across all disciplines;
- National Energy Research Institute - formulation of a National Energy R&D Strategy, and flagship research programmes.

National Science and Technology Forum

Excerpt from NSTF website:

One of the groups involved in South Africa's landmark CODESA Convention was the Science and Technology Working Group. As a result of the findings and recommendations of this group, Government founded the National Science and Technology Forum (NSTF) in 1995 to oversee implementation.

The Forum was established against the background of the Government of National Unity's Reconstruction and Development Programme. The challenge is to oversee the restructuring of South Africa's national science system and to ensure an integrated approach to science and technology.

The Minister of Arts, Culture, Science and Technology (ACST), made his intention clear by recognising the then National Science and Technology Initiative as a Science and Technology (S&T) Forum for purposes of consultation and addressing S&T issues within the broad S&T community.

On 28 March 1995, the first plenary meeting of the NSTF was opened by the Minister of ACST. The mandate given to the NSTF by government was that it should act as the sounding board, communication channel and constructive watchdog of S&T in South Africa. Integral to this mandate is the need to establish best practice norms, and to integrate and share the good and positive advancements currently being made in the fields of Science, Engineering and Technology (SET).

As the sounding-board, communications channel and constructive watchdog of Science and Technology at implementation level, the NSTF enjoys the mentorship of influential leaders like President Thabo Mbeki and the Minister of ACST,

Dr Ben Ngubane, and support from stakeholders at all levels, from the smallest of businesses, through all levels of education, to government.

Southern African Association of Science and Technology Centres (SAASTEC)

The vision of SAASTEC is to facilitate in creating a technologically-based Southern African society which will ensure a competitive edge in the global economy. Their Mission is to contribute to the improvement of life of Southern African nations by improving scientific knowledge and skills through:

- the utilisation of interactive living science and technology discovery centres (S&T centres),
- to disseminate knowledge in science and technology to the public in general and the youth in particular through imaginative and enjoyable hands-on exhibits, displays and programmes, so that they can appreciate the relevance of science and technology in their daily lives,
- to serve as a catalyst for our youth to develop their creativity and to nurture their interest in related fields,
- to establish a centre of excellence and innovation in non-formal science education, and
- to provide satisfying careers for the S&T centre workforce.

The Aims and Objectives are:

- to stimulate interest in S&T centres,
- to establish more S&T centres in rural areas,
- to investigate and support mobile centres and transportable units.
- to stimulate ideas in the design of new exhibits.
- to hold regular workshops and meetings in different centres.

- to evaluate the impact of S&T centres.
- to establish contact with industry.
- to establish links with international bodies.
- to address the issue of funding.
- to provide training in the management of S&T centres.
- to encourage the sharing of resources.
- to develop a national marketing strategy.
- to provide a national network of information interchange between S&T centres.
- to have a joint voice that is nationally recognized, to lobby government and industry.

The Education aims and objectives are:

- to promote S&T in schools.
- to link S&T centres to the formal education structure.
- to stimulate interest in careers in S&T.
- to encourage workshops and courses aimed at upgrading science teachers' practical teaching skills.
- to encourage the formation of science clubs.

The Community aims and objectives are:

- to promote technology and the natural and physical sciences in general.
- to ensure that S&T centres are linked to the broader community.
- to promote S&T awareness and literacy.
- to establish 'S&T routes' for school groups or tourists to visit.
- to encourage visits from non-traditional visitors.

Trends and Overview of Existing Science Centres

Growth and Development Trends

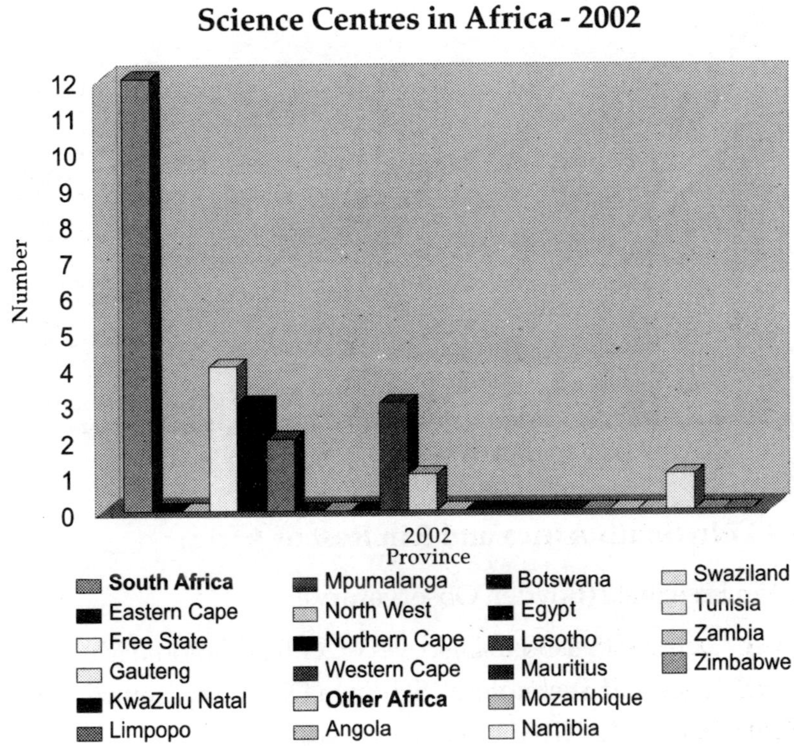

2002 - 12 in South Africa, 1 in Rest of Africa

- 4 in Gauteng (FEST, UP Discovery Centre, Gold Reef City, HARTRAO)
- 3 in KwaZulu-Natal (Unizul SC, Old Mutual-MTN ScienCentre, Olwazini)
- 3 in Western Cape (MTN ScienCentre, Telkom Exploratorium, Ithemba Science Centre at NAC)
- 2 in Limpopo Province (University of the North SC, Giyani SC)
- 1 in Tunis

Science Centres in Africa - 2006

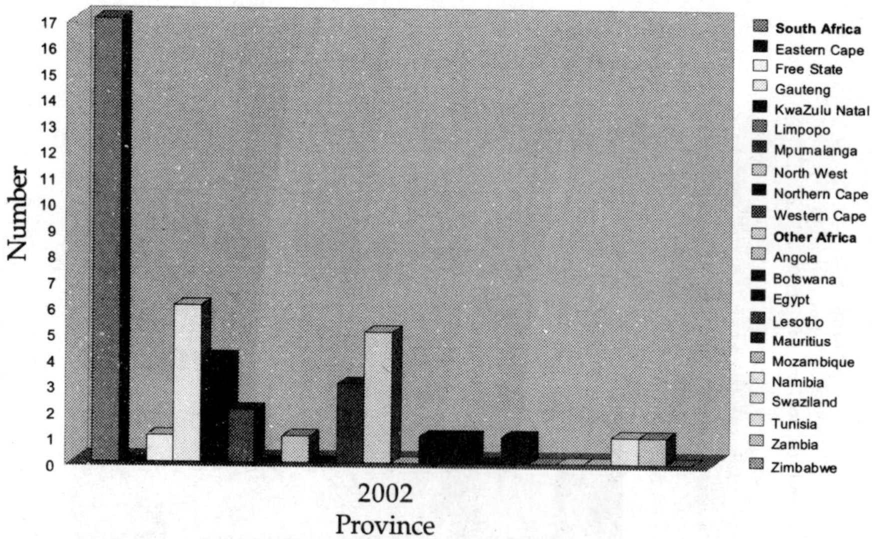

2006 - 17 in South Africa and 5 in Rest of Africa

- 1 in Free State (Boyden Observatory)
- 6 in Gauteng (Sci-Bono Discovery Centre, National Museum of Science and Technology, Sci-Enza Discovery Centre, Gold Reef City, HARTRAO, Transvaal Museum SC)
- 4 in KwaZulu-Natal (Unizul SC, Old Mutual MTN ScienCentre, Olwazini, Kwazuzulwazi SC,)
- 2 in Limpopo Province (Univ. of the North SC, Giyani SC)
- 1 in North West (Potchefstroom University)
- 3 in Western Cape (MTN ScienCentre, Ithemba SC at NAC, Hermanus Magnetic Observatory (Telkom Exploratorium closed))
- 1 in Botswana (Botech)
- 1 in Egypt (Cairo SC)
- 1 in Mauritius (Mauritius SC)

- 1 in Tunisia (Tunis SC)
- 1 in Zambia (National SC)

It can be seen that there is a growth trend for the establishment of science centres. In the next section the number of planned science centres is detailed, and this indicates how the growth trend is escalating.

Proposed Network of Science Centres

The DST published in 2005 a document defining the Norms and Standards for the Development of a Network of Science Centres in South Africa.

The draft document noted above was presented to NAM SC Conference in Hanoi in 2004 by Mr. Lebs Mpahlele

The Policy and Budget for the Development of a Network of Science Centres has not yet been submitted to Cabinet for Approval

This is affecting the future growth of science centres in South Africa.

Science Centre Statistics

This section was presented by Mr Alfred Tsipa, President of SAASTEC (Southern African Association of Science and Technology Centres) and Head of Programmes at Unizul Science Centre. The statistics have been prepared by Prof. Mike Bruton of MTN Sciencentre (presented in the Appendix).

What is an Interactive Science Centre?

"A permanently established educational facility that has specifically been created to facilitate interactive teaching and learning".

Challenges Facing South African Science Centres

Government Recognition

There is lack of recognition by government of the role science centres play in Human Capital Development. This role is not only a direct formal education role, but the informal education role, and the key role of creating an enabling environment for science technology engineering and mathematics, and other life skills and lifelong learning.

Credibility

Science Centres lack credibility by investors / sponsors in their ability to deliver informal science education, contribute to human capital development, and to provide the necessary returns for corporate social investment, public relations and marketing.

Lack of Capacity

There is a significant lack of capacity of skills required to manage and operate science centres, in South Africa, and for the future proposed network.

Sustainability

The model of a network of small less sophisticated science centres located in outlying and rural areas is a cost effective development cost / CAPEX (capital expenditure) solution. This model however would require a much greater level of subsidisation for OPEX (operating expenditure), possibly total subsidisation - the small rural science centres will find it difficult to generate own income.

The model of larger more sophisticated science centres located in urban nodes, will require significant development cost/CAPEX (capital expenditure). The model however would be more self-sustaining in that the science centre can self-generate a substantial portion of the OPEX through entrepreneurial activities.

The most significant operational cost is the transport costs of learners to a science centre located in an urban node - as much as 40% of operational cost.

Underdeveloped Exhibit Manufacturing Industry

The exhibit development and manufacturing industry is not yet established in South Africa, and there are many problems associated with the procurement of exhibits locally. The procurement of exhibits from abroad are expensive.

Science Centre Development Strategies

Science Centre Conceptual Models

The diagram above describes the components of a science centre. The facilities include a science exhibition area where not only are the interactive exhibits displayed, but also provides the venue and facilities for many of the programmes and activities, a resource centre which includes laboratories, libraries and classrooms where

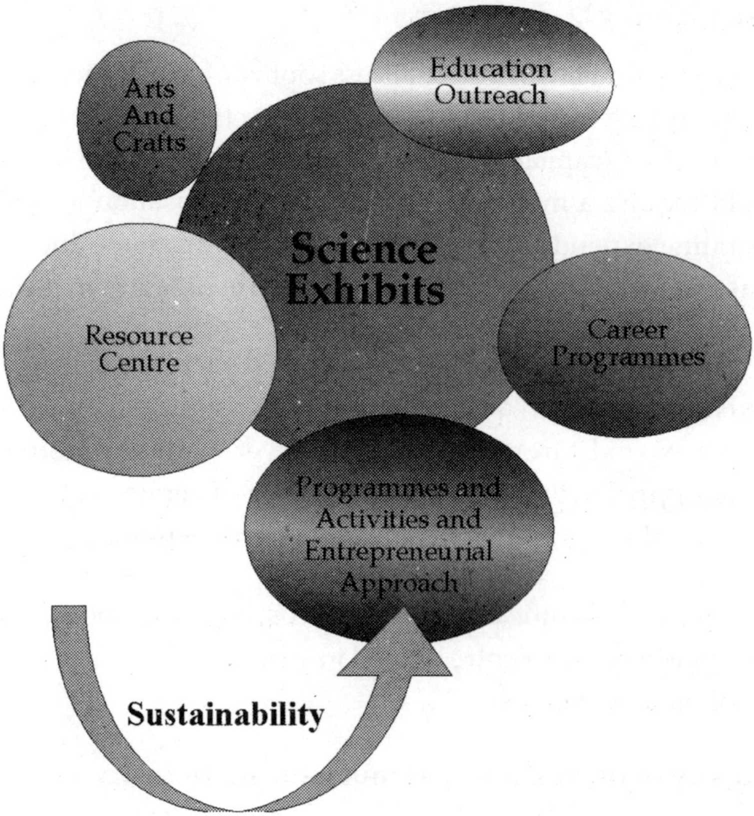

formal education programmes can be supported, and a career centre where career advisory and support programmes can be located. The science centre requires outreach programmes where the staff of the science centre travel from the science centre to outlying areas to host various science centre programmes. An important medium of science communication is art and craft, and performing arts and facilities and programmes should be included.

The underlying sustainability of all these components is achieved through the balance between the various components (Programmes; Facilities; Exhibits; Career Programmes; Outreach; Arts and Crafts and an entrepreneurial operating approach)

Development Processes

The development of a science centre can be split into a number of stages:

Concept Proposal

As with all projects it is important to develop a concept proposal and statement of need for the project at the outset.

Stakeholder Consultation

- Understanding a Science Centre: key to the stakeholder and potential sponsor consultation is to educate the parties as to the mission and objectives of a science centre and the benefits it can generate.
- Department of Education: the local department of education are a key stakeholder, and it is advisable to solicit their buyin to the project.
- Buy-in: it is important to get all stakeholders and potential sponsors to buy-in to the project as soon as possible.

Business Case

- Feasibility: the feasibility study includes any market research that is required, develops a project design for both the programmes and activities, and the facilities, and undertakes the technical research required to develop CAPEX, OPINC and OPEX Budgets, management and operational structures.
- Sustainability: the Business Case then reviews the feasibility study and presents a sustainable case.
- Development Framework: a development framework is then drawn up outlining the development thrusts and processes

required including fundraising, programme development, facilities construction, exhibit development and procurement, communication strategies, and management appointments etc.

Impact Assessment

The development of an early impact assessment hypothesis quantifying the educational and economic returns is useful in promoting the project and securing funding and sponsorship.

Legal Structuring

It is advantageous to structure the science centre vehicle both legally and financially at an early stage, whether this be a not for profit organisation, public benefit organisation, Section 21 company, Section 18A Trust or other appropriate vehicle.

Implementation

The implementation stage covers the delivery of all issues for the successful development.

Implementation Strategies

Implementation strategies cover the following thrusts as described in the following diagram and can include the support of the client team in various areas:

Development Challenges

Development challenges include:

- Securing Political and Stakeholder Support;
- Sustainability;
- Fundraising and Funding Strategies;

- Economic and Education Impact Assessment;
- Theming and Exhibits;
- Exhibit Procurement;
- Management Capacity;

Generic Project Implementation Structure

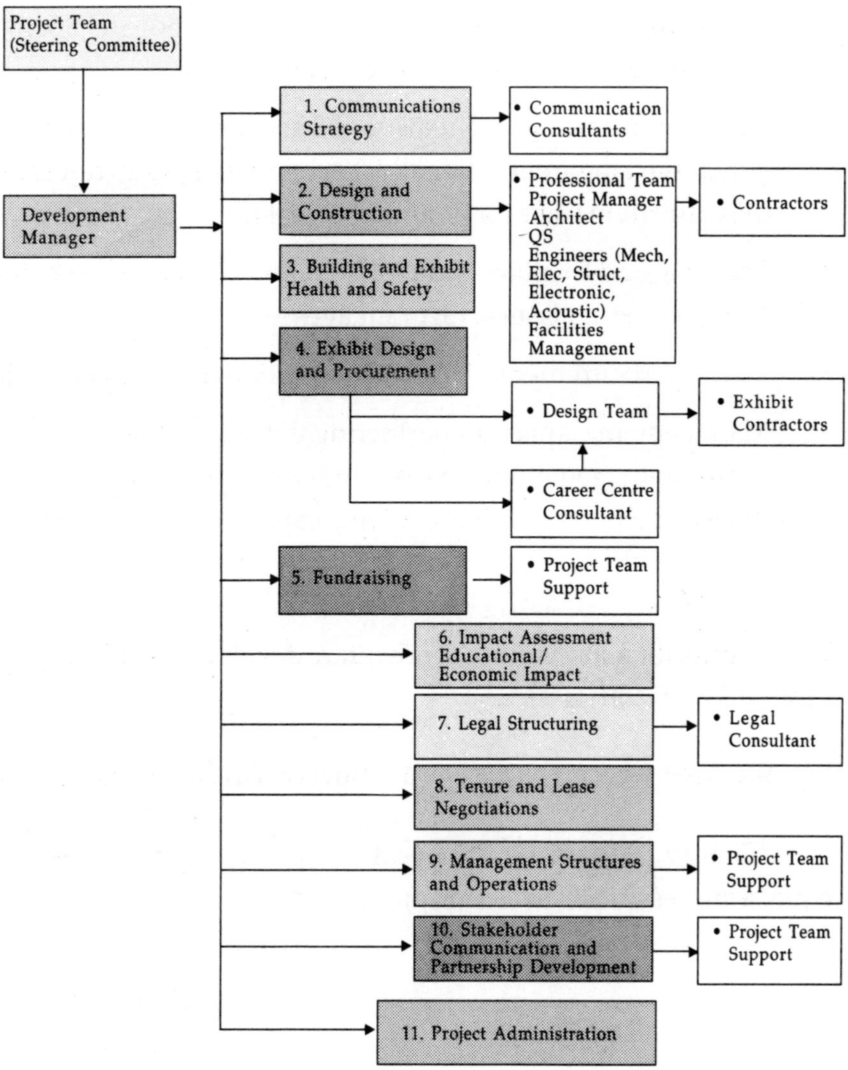

Strategies to Address the Challenges

The following strategies are suggested for addressing the development challenges:

- Political Support - Education Department buy-in, Partnership with Education Department
- Sustainability – Business Case, Income Generation Facilities
- Fundraising – Development of CSI (Corporate Social Investment) and Marketing Packages
- EIA (Economic / Educational Impact Assessment) – Benchmarking Internationally. Early projections to develop the Education Case for potential investors
- Theming and Exhibits – Integrated Plan – Curriculum, Social and Contextual Issues, EIA Linkages
- Exhibit Procurement – Design led rather than contractor led
- Management Capacity – partnering with established science centre management teams, or medium term outsourcing to development consultants allowing capacity to be developed.

Conclusion

The formula for a successful science centre development (Courtesy: Prof. Mike Bruton) is:

E^3 + \$ x (106) + G^2 + H^2O + ~ + ü = Successful Science Centre!!

(Energy, Dollars, Graft, Sweat, Inspiration and Experience equal a successful science centre).

References

- Department of Science and Technology: Republic of South Africa: Corporate Strategy 2005/6 - 2008/10
- Department of Science and Technology: Republic of South Africa: (Nov 04) Proposed National Norms and Standards for a Network of Science Centres in South Africa
- Department of Education: Republic of South Africa: (Sept-04) The Development of Education - Country Report of South Africa - 47th Conference on Education Sept-04
- Department of Education and Labour: Republic of South Africa: (2000) Human Resource Development Strategy for South Africa
- Department of Education: Republic of South Africa: 2000 School Register of Needs
- National Science and Technology Forum: Annual Report 2005
- Southern African Association of Science and Technology Centres: Jan-06 Website

APPENDIX

Interactive Science Centres in Africa

This section was presented by Mr Alfred Tsipa, President of SAASTEC (Southern African Association of Science and Technology Centres) and Head of Programmes at Unizul Science Centre. The statistics have been prepared by Prof. Mike Bruton of MTN Sciencentre.

Science Centres in Africa

22 (Africa); 18 (South Africa)

- 3 in Western Cape (MTN ScienCentre, Ithemba Labs Science Centre, Hermanus Magnetic Observatory)
- 4 in KwaZulu-Natal (Unizul SC, Kwazuzulwazi SC, Old Mutual MTN Science Centre, Olwazini)
- 7 in Gauteng (Sci-Bono, National Museum of Science and Technology, Sci-Enza Discovery Centre, Gold Reef City, HARTRAO, RAU Technolab, Transvaal Museum SC, Sterkfontein??)
- 2 in Northern Province (Univ. of the North SC, Giyani SC)
- 1 in North West (Potchefstroom University)
- 1 in Free State (Boyden Observatory)
- Other Africa
- 1 in Botswana (Botswana Technology Centre)
- Possibly 1 in Egypt
- 1 in Mauritius
- 1 in Tunisia (Tunis)
- Others?

Mobile Science Centres in South Africa

1. Discoverymobile of the Gateway Discovery Trust, Cape Town
2. University of Limpopo Mobile Unit – Polokwane
3. Emasondosondo Mobile Unit - Sci-Bono-Gauteng
4. Tsebo Koloing of the University of Pretoria

Location of Existing Science Centres

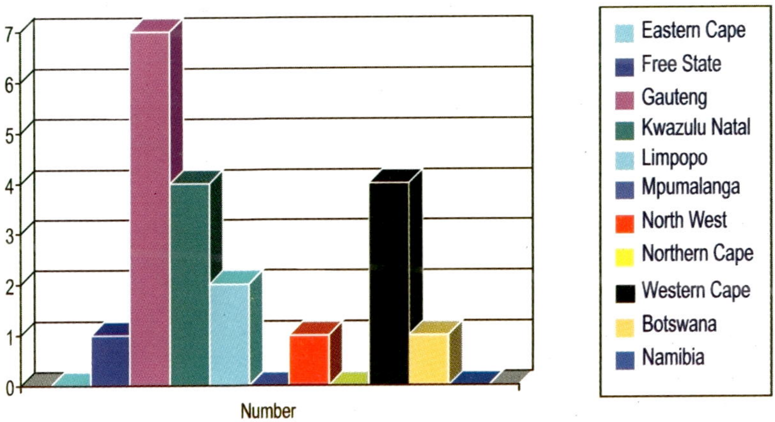

Future Science Centres in Southern Africa

1. 4 in Western Cape (Koeberg, Thunder City, Cango Caves, Peninsula NP)
2. 3 in Gauteng (Menlyn Park, MTN HQ, Vaal Triangle Tech)
3. 1 in the Northern Cape (Sutherland)
4. 3 in the Eastern Cape (East London, Uitenhage, Bayworld PE)
5. 1 in KwaZulu-Natal (Stanger)
6. 2 in the Free State (Sasolburg, Bloemfontein)
7. 0 in Limpopo Province, North West or Mpumalanga
8. 2 in Namibia (Otjiwarango?)
9. Others?

Location of Future Science Centres

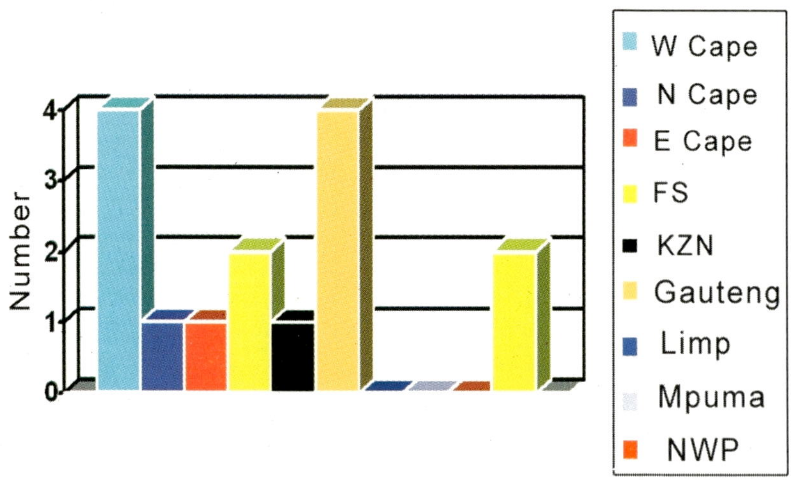

Demographic Environment

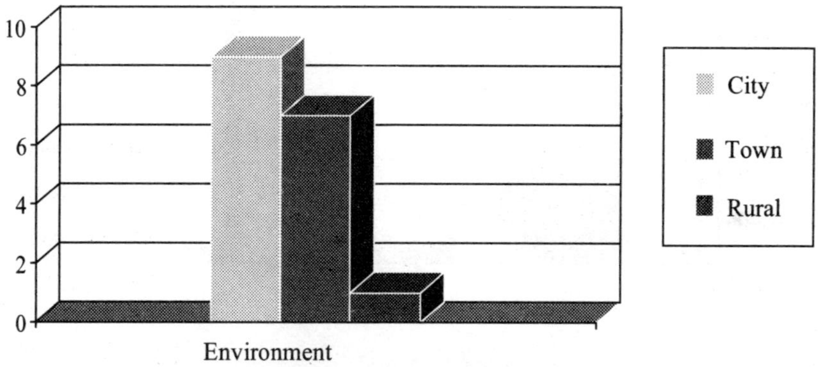

Years since Establishment

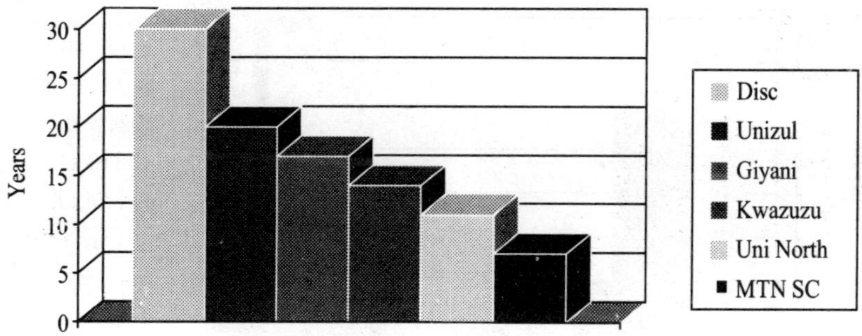

Affiliation

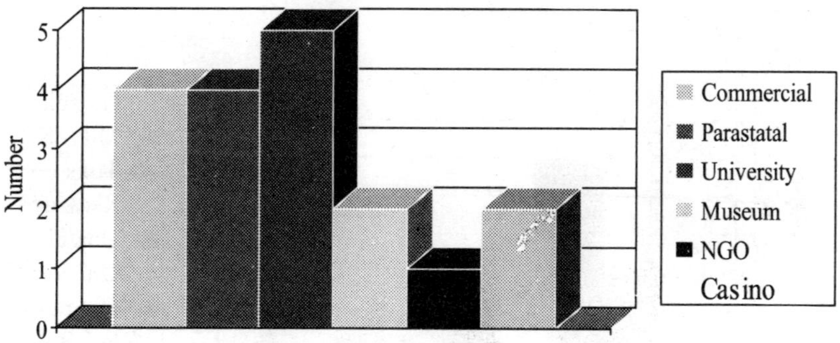

Total Floor Areas

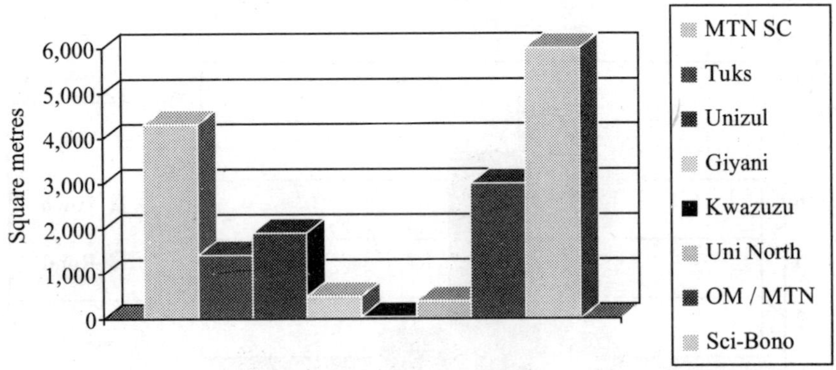

Number of Staff

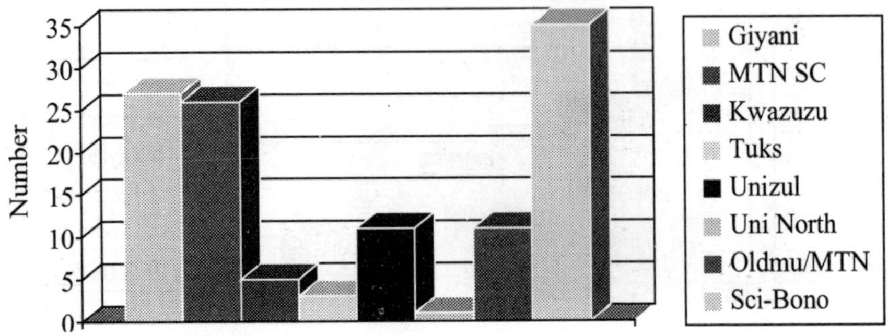

Number of Educators

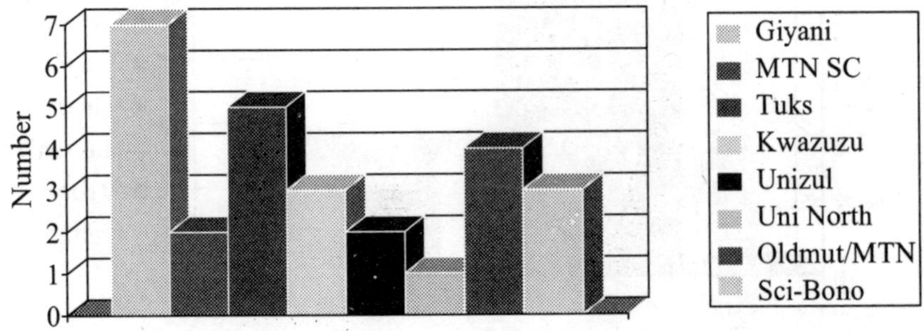

Annual Visitation Rates

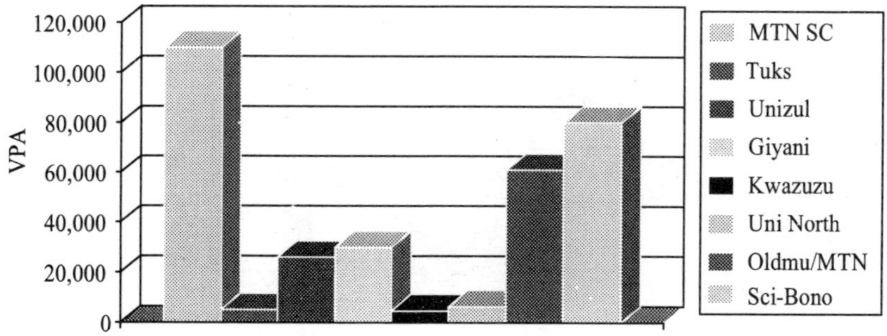

Percentage of Visitors in School Groups

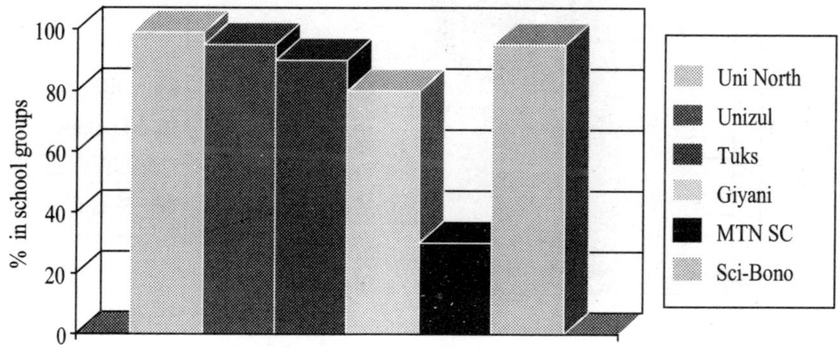

Percentage of Visitors < 18 yrs

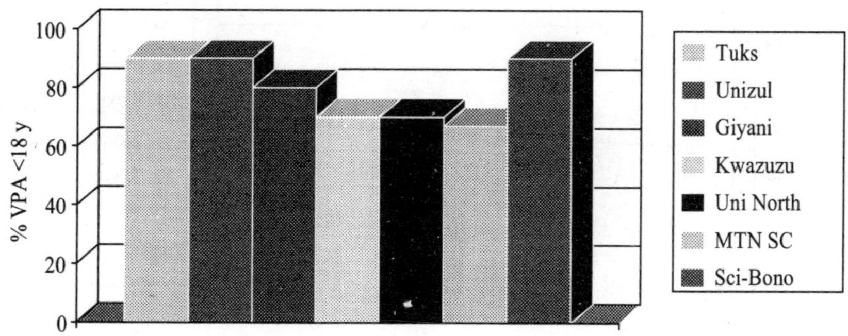

Total Budget Per Year

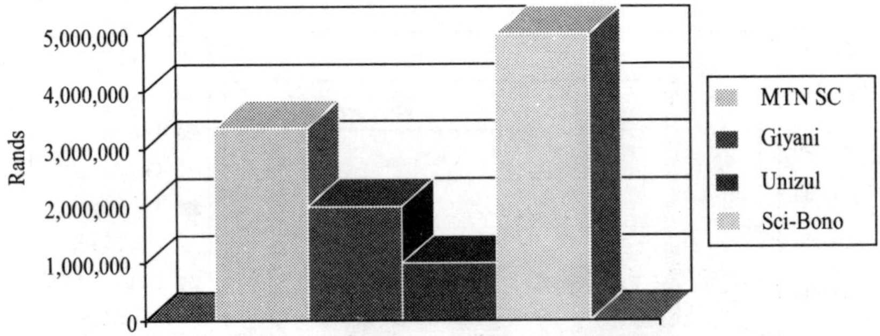

Educational Focus

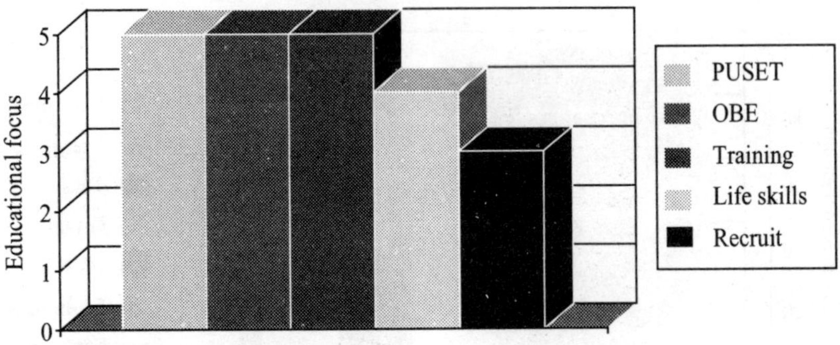

Auditorium Seating Capacity

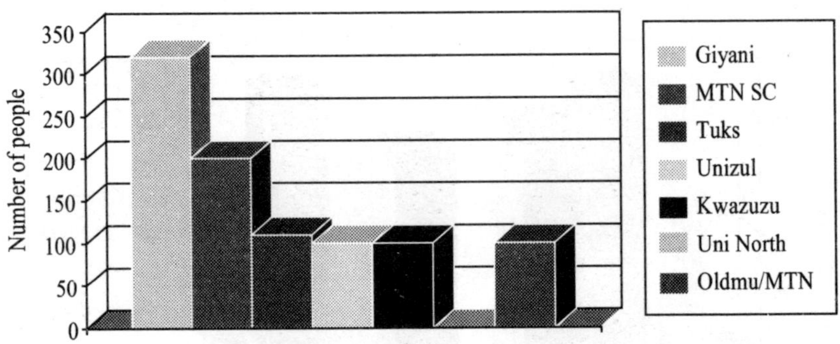

Number of Training / Exhibit Computers

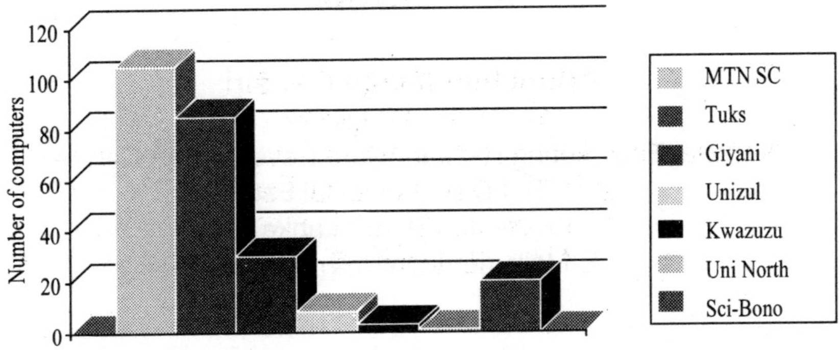

Museums and Science Centres in Sri Lanka

Arumahennadige Piyasiri
Mechanical Engineer,
National Engineering Research and Development Centre,
2P/17B, I.D.B., Industrial Estate,
Ekala, Ja-Ela (Sri Lanka)
E-Mail: nerdcentre@nerdc.lk

Abstract

Sri Lanka, an island in the Indian Ocean and located south of the Indian subcontinent, is also known as the Pearl of the Indian Ocean.

The country's literacy rate is 90-93%, which is one of the highest in Asia. Present and past all governments elected have taken several steps to strengthen the science knowledge among people.

The education system of Sri Lanka has highly considered the Science and Mathematics as compulsory subjects to all students from grade 6 to grade 11. After success of G.C.E. (O/L) examination, the student is free to select the subjects for higher education including Science subjects.

Regional and national level science competitions are held annually. Annual Presidential awards for young inventors, scientists at the national level have been organized through Sri Lanka Inventors' Commission, Institution for Engineers of Sri Lanka etc.

The Ministry of Science and Technology of Sri Lanka has initiated the program for popularization of Science in the country through Science and Technology Centres attached to all divisional secretariats. The ministry has opened 65 Vidatha centres during year 2005.

The museums are the places to discover, explore and test ideas about the natural world. In Sri Lanka too, they are situated in all parts of the country. The National Museum situated in capital City Colombo was established in 1877 having collection of antiques, national treasures and artifacts from all parts of island. Other museums display artifacts, fauna and flora of the sea and environment, gems, a model displaying the process of gem-mining, archeological museums etc.

In addition the NERDC of Sri Lanka under Ministry of Science and Technology has established the country's first and only Science and Technological Park to uplift the science among people in order to improve the creativity of the people. And also the NERDC has started construction of country's first Engineering Museum to display the ancient technologies developed by our forefathers. Presently, the scientists and the engineers are working together for making / fabricating interactive exhibits for the museum.

Keywords: NERDC (National Engineering Research & Development Centre), Engineering, Inventions, Innovations, Province, Creativity, Vidatha (Science and technology centres set up by Ministry of Science & Technology).

Introduction

A teardrop-shaped island just off the southern tip of the Indian sub continent, less than 50 km. (31 miles) away at its closest, Sri

Lanka has links with the cultures of India that stretch back beyond history, but it would be a mistake to think of it as an India in miniature.

Sri Lanka lies between 5° 55' and 9° 55' north of the equator and between the eastern longitudes 79° 42' and 81° 52'. The climate of Sri Lanka is typically tropical with an average temperature of 27°C. In the higher elevations it can be quite cool with temperatures going down to 16°C at an altitude of nearly 2,000 metres.

Mainly an agricultural country, the chief crop of Sri Lanka is rice with which the country is almost self-sufficient. Tea, rubber and coconut are also important agricultural crops, with tea being a major foreign exchange earner. Other crops of importance are cocoa and spices. Sri Lanka is also a major exporter of precious and semi-precious stones. In the last three decades tourism has emerged as an important industry.

From North to South it has a maximum length of 435 km (270 miles) and at its widest point it measures 225 km. (140 miles), giving it a land area of 65,600 sq.km. (25,000 sq.miles). This entire stretch encompasses beautiful tropical beaches, verdant vegetation, ancient monuments and a thousand delights to please all tastes. Bright, sunny, warm days are the rule and are common even during the height of the monsoon - climatically Sri Lanka has no off season.

Sri Lanka has a recorded history of over 2500 years. Although there is some evidence that the island was inhabited since prehistoric times, it is believed that the advent of Vijaya, an Indian Prince with his 700 followers in 543 B.C. laid the foundation of the Sinhala race which constitutes the majority of the population of the country today.

The next major event in the island's history was the arrival in 307 B.C. of the Buddha's disciple Arahath Mahinda, son of Emperor Asoka the great of India, with the teachings of Lord Buddha. The noble message of the Buddha has run strongly through more than 2500 years of the religion and history of the island. Compassion that the Buddha taught has influenced the way of life of the people over the centuries. Irrigation, too occupied an unique position in ancient Sri Lanka. The Island was then known as the 'Granary of the East'.

In 1505 the Portuguese arrived in *Colombo* and gained a monopoly on the invaluable spice and cinnamon trade. Later, the Dutch arrived and were more interested in trade and profits than religion or land, although they too unsuccessfully tried to bring the *Kandyan* kingdom under their control. The British arrived in 1796. In 1815, the British became the first European power to rule the entire island. The work of empire moved inexorably forward as roads were built, coffee, tea, cinnamon and coconut plantations sprang up and English was introduced as the national language. By a process of peaceful constitutional evolution, Sri Lanka won independence in 1948. Sri Lanka became a Republic in 1972 with the adoption of a new constitution.

For about 350 years of pre independence period, foreign nationals have established several museums such as National Museum, Dutch Museum etc in the country. Museums such as Weera Puran Appu Museum and Bandaranaike Museum were established in post independence period.

Government Involvement

The government is spending a vast amount of money for free education and free health in Sri Lanka. Therefore, the Index of physical quality of Life and the Literacy rates are much higher compared to other developing countries in the world. From year

2005 onwards the government of Democratic Socialist Republic of Sri Lanka has increased the budgetary allocation to Ministry of Science and Technology for popularisation of science and technology. The Presidential Award system for junior inventors has been initiated and the award winners are sent for participation in international competitions and events with the government assistance through the Inventors' Commission.

Role of the Education Ministry

The education system of Sri Lanka makes it compulsory to study Science and Mathematics for all students from grade 6 to grade 11. After success of G.C.E. (O/L) examination, the student is free to select the subjects for higher education including Science subjects. The ministry has initiated the program to provide laboratory facilities, library facilities, and computer facilities including trained teachers for all the government schools with the assistance of foreign funding organizations.

Role of the Science and Technology Ministry

Under the Ministry of Science and Technology, there are a number of institutions and science centres established in all parts of the country. During the year 2005, the ministry has allocated SLR 300 Million for establishment of 100 VIDATHA Centres under the Divisional Secretariats. Through these centres, the ministry is promoting the science and technological innovations designed and developed by the institutions coming under the Ministry.

Science Centres and Museums of Sri Lanka

Science centres and museum are unique resources for internal learning, a process central to forging knowledge, skills and positive attitudes. They are the places to discover, explore and test ideas about the natural world. According to an unnamed Scientist "Science

Centres are places where people of all ages can learn at their own pace, engage their curiosity, use their senses to ask and answer questions and explain to others what they have learned". Science Centres play a unique role in the community, the school and the home in the educational infrastructure, one that can propel science educational reforms in the 21st century.

Museums of Sri Lanka

The National Museum, Colombo

The National Museum is situated at Sir Marcus Fernando Mawatha, Colombo 07. The first public Museum was established in Sri Lanka (1877). Best known for its collection of antiques and objects d'art displaying the cultural heritage of Sri Lanka. It includes the national treasures and artefacts from all parts of the island. A section of the first floor houses the Puppetry and Children's Museum. It also houses a library with a collection of about 500,000 books including very valuable and rare ones and more than 4,000 ancient palm leaf manuscripts.

The National Museum of Natural History

The National Museum of Natural History, behind the main museum, has many fine specimens of Sri Lanka's wildlife and other natural resources.

The museum's paintings, dating back to several centuries, tells a tale of a bygone era when the pace was more relaxed. There are scenes of Sri Lanka's aborigines, the Veddahs, hunting with bows and arrows.

For researchers, the Museum Library has over half a million publications of interest. For children, the fascinating world of puppetry comes alive on the first floor. There are masks used in traditional dance, including devil dancing.

The National Museum of Natural History is situated in the same premises as the Cultural Museum. It displays the Natural Heritage of Sri Lanka. The fauna i.e. the mammals and the birds are displayed in dioramas. There are sections on Applied Botany, Geology and Fossils and the Natural Environment. In the Discovery Room one finds the mounted skeleton of an elephant and a scale model in relief showing the topography of a part of Sri Lanka.

The Dutch Period Museum, Colombo

The Dutch Period Museum in the old "Dutch House" on Prince Street, Pettah, (Colombo 11), which houses this museum was built in the latter part of the 17th century and was initially the residence of Count August Carl Van Ranzow along with five other houses of the elite. Today, the sides of the street are choc-a-block with boutiques and stores of Moslem traders. The restoration of this building commenced in 1977 was completed in 1981. This museum was opened to the public in 1982. This building embodies the unique architectural features of a colonial Dutch town house. The museum while displaying the Dutch legacy with the artefacts viz. furniture, ceramics, coins, arms etc. portrays facets of contemporary life and culture.

The Museum, Kandy

The Museum, Kandy is situated behind the Temple of the Tooth, in a building of historical and architectural interest. The collections are all of the Kandyan Period (17th – 18th Century).

The National Gem Museum, Ratnapura

The National Gem Museum of Ratnapura is housed in the famous Ehelapola Walawwa on the Colombo Road in Ratnapura. The museum displays to a great extent the prehistory of Sri Lanka. Ratnapura being famous for gems, the process of gem-mining is displayed through a model. Some of the artefacts displayed here, reflect the unique arts & culture of the Sabaragamuwa Province.

The Folk Museum, Anuradhapura

The Folk Museum is in the sacred city close to the Archaeological Museum and has a collection of artefacts illustrative of the rural life of the North Central Province.

Museum, Galle

The Museum is situated within the Fort of Galle in the Dutch Colonial building. In Church Street is the Cultural Museum adjoining the New Oriental Hotel. The artefacts reflect the art and culture of the Southern Province.

The National Maritime Museum, Galle

The National Maritime Museum is located within the Fort of Galle in a colonial Dutch warehouse with imposing pillars. This Museum displays the organisms from the sea and the environment. Artefacts consist of preserved material and scale models of whales and fishes. All the resources of the sea are covered in this Museum. It also houses dioramas with life sized models, and the traditional methods of fishing. Some artefacts of underwater archaeology are on display. An interesting experiment is the "walk-into -the sea" diorama, showing the natural coral beds, sea grass beds and deep-sea fishes. Finally, one leaves the museum seeing the causes of sea pollution, coast erosion and methods used to combat these problems.

Weera Puran Appu Museum, Moratuwa

Weera Puran Appu Museum is housed at Weera Puran Appu Vidyalaya, New Galle Road, Moratuwa. This Museum exhibits items in relation to the life and time of this great hero who fought the British against unfair levy of taxes and injustice and laid down his life in defence of the country.

Bandaranaike Museum, Colombo

Bandaranaike Museum is housed in the Bandaranaike Memorial International Conference Hall, Bauddhaloka Mawatha, Colombo 07. The museum contains photographs, objects and documents portraying the life and times of the late Prime Minister, S W R D Bandaranaike. Visitors can listen to recordings of some of his famous speeches.

Archaeological Museums

The Archaeological Department has established Archaeological Site Museums in Anuradhapura (Ancient city). Isurumuniya, Minintale, Veheragala, Vavyniya, Jaffna, Sigiriya, Kandy, Dedigama, Yapahuwa, Paduwasnuwara, Kotte, Matara (Star-Fort), Deegavapiya and Kataragama. Archaeological Museums are open daily from 0800 hrs. to 1700 hrs. But closed on Tuesdays and some of them will be closed on public holidays too.

Science Centres in Sri Lanka

Vidatha Centres:

Vidatha Centres are the Science & Technology Centres which have been established by the Ministry of Science & Technology. The Ministry has initiated to set up the Science and Technology Centres all over the island. In the first stage, there will be Science Centres attached to all divisional secretariats. To date there are about 65 Centres established in some divisional secretariats such as Badulla, Kandy, Hambantota etc,. The people can visit the Vidatha centres and study the exhibits available there. For them to learn, there are newly recruited science graduates. If the people need to start a self employment project through these exhibits, they will be trained and fabricate the product developed by the relevant institute.

In addition to the Vidatha Centres, the ministry has arranged a special train equipped with some of the Science and Technological equipments in the compartments to display the Science concepts to the visitors to the exhibition train. This Science train is parked at a railway stations for sometime during which the interested people can visit the train for improving their Science knowledge.

NERDC Science and Technology Park

The National Engineering Research and Development Centre of Sri Lanka was established in 1974. To celebrate the Silver Jubilee of the centre in 1999, the NERDC Science and Technology Park was set up in the same premises. The area covered by the park is 4.5 acres. The NERDC science and Technology Park is the one and only Technology Park in Sri Lanka

Aims and Objectives:

The main objectives for setting up of the Park were to:

1. Enhance the creativity of the students and youth leading to inventions and innovations
2. Upgrade and popularize the knowledge of Science and Technology among Sri Lankan public
3. Guide towards self employment opportunities
4. Improve productivity using energy efficient systems
5. Give value for domestic and industrial waste
6. Window for NERDC activities at a glance

Products/ Services offered by NERDC S&T Park:

To achieve above aims and objectives NERDC Science & Technology Park offers following services to the visitors visiting to the park.

- Making aware of the,
  - (i) History of the NERD Centre
  - (ii) Inventions/Technologies/Processes developed by Sri Lanka
  - (iii) Advantages of inventions/innovations to the individuals/organizations/ groups as well as to the country
  - (iv) And the benefits to the country and to the individuals who creates innovations.
- Making aware of
  - (i) NERDC developed products / technologies/Processes
  - (ii) NERDC services offered to the public such as construction of cost effective buildings, energy audits, consultant services, training programs conducted and CME activities etc.
- Displaying the practical demonstrations of NERD developed products and processes to the visitors. In addition we sell the same products to the interested parties through Sales Unit.
- Teaching the Science concepts and technologies developed at NERDC to visitors.
- Helping the G.C.E Advanced Level students to gather information for their project report.
- Motivating the people for self-employment.

- Accommodation facilities to the students and teachers from far away places, trainees who register for in-house NERD training programs / seminars etc.
- Canteen facilities, resting and first aid facilities for the visitors to the Technology Park and occupants of the Hostel.

Currently, the NERDC Science & Technology Park exhibits and demonstrates the Technological products/ process/ projects which have been designed and developed by NERDC engineers and scientists since 1974. Majority of the exhibits available in the park are in the fields of Renewable Energy, Agricultural Engineering, Civil Engineering, Environmental Engineering, Electrical & Electronic Engineering. In addition there are exhibits which are specially designed for G.C.E ordinary level students in grade 11.

Exhibits:

Exhibits display in the S&T Park belongs to the following Engineering Departments.

Civil Engineering - Cost effective Civil construction technologies are displayed. They are;

- Construction of cost effective foundation
- Cost effective wall constructions (slip form wall construction technique)
- Construction of door and window frames from concrete
- Pre cast pre-stress column fabrication
- Beam fabrication
- Slab construction using pre stress trapezoidal beams
- Cost effective roof constructions
- Cost effective buildings

Renewable Energy - Department displays the products and processes of Solar Energy, Wind Energy, Bio Mass Energy etc.

- Solar dryers, stills, concentrator, water heaters etc
- Wind mill water pump, wind mill electricity generators
- Fire wood gassifiers for thermal and electrical
- generation applications , saw dust operated bakery ovens
- Bio-gas digesters

Agricultural Engineering - Department displays the products as follows

- Paddy storage bin
- Coconut oil expellers
- Cinnamon oil distillation
- Coconut de-husker
- Parboiled paddy mill
- Raw Paddy Mill

Electrical & Electronics - Department displays following exhibits:

- Electronic ballast
- Fan regulator
- Induction motor
- Teaching aids (mini lab)
- Computer aided teaching
- Electricity generation through solar panels

For whom: PLACE/Customer Segment

At the beginning our main target audiences to the Technology Park were school students and teachers. Due to the popularity and all works of people such as students from schools, technical colleges, agricultural schools, private educational institutes, international schools, universities etc and parents, industrialists, unemployed, underemployed have become our regular visitors in the Technology Park. In addition the people from non-governmental organizations, women organizations, staff/ field officers from banks are frequently visiting the Park.

For promotion and publicity, the means used are as follows:

1. Word of mouth
2. Letters mailed to schools
3. Customers who are interested in purchasing NERD developed products
4. Television programs, News paper articles, exhibitions, awareness programs etc.
5. Accommodation facilities to visitors provided by Hostel building constructed at Technology Park premises.
6. Exhibition of newly developed products by NERD Centre.

Table I–Visitors arrival since 1999 August

YEAR	**Visitors Arrival**
1999 Aug-Dec	3043
2000	6813
2001	13511
2002	20938
2003	21575.
2004	21758
2005	16139

As the visitors arrival to the Technology Park has been increased annually (see table I), the services offered by the Technology Park to the visitors also have been improved. The construction of Hostel facilities for the far away schools and newly constructed canteen facilities have contributed to the increased inflow. The Centre has not promoted the Technology Park through electronic media yet. If it is done so, the visitors arrival can be increased manifold.

Planned activities for year 2006

1. To provide accommodation for the students and teachers who visit to the Technology Park from far away schools
2. To provide better facilities such as canteen facilities, toilet facilities etc by which we expect to increase the visitors to the park.
3. To provide Hostel facilities for the trainees, resource personnel who engage with NERD in-house training programs
4. To provide facilities for the Resource personals/supervisors from overseas institutions to the NERD Centre
5. To sell brochures, other booklets to the visitors.
6. To exhibit new projects/process replacing older exhibits at least once in two months period.

Strategies to increase the visitors to the Science and Technology Park

1. Mailing a letter to all schools Principals, Technical Colleges, Samurdi Groups etc.
2. Promotion of the Technology Park activities through Divisional Secretariats and Local Government Bodies such as local government authorities.
3. Promotion through a paper advertisement.
4. Exhibiting new projects/processes replacing old items at least once in two months.

5. Presently, science education curriculum for year 8,9,10 and 11 consists with the concepts of teaching aids and other science & technology concepts introduced at the Technology Park. We can get the maximum benefit through this opportunity to increase the inflow of students to Technology Park.
6. Construction of first of the proposed NERC Engineering Museum to display past achievements of our great Sri Lankan forefathers.

Proposed NERDC Engineering Museum

In addition, National Engineering Research & Development Centre has embarked in setting up of a Centre to display past achievement of our great Sri Lankans as we do not have in Sri Lanka an Engineering Park nor an Engineering museum. The establishment of facility of this nature could be a tremendous encouragement for the visitors to the present Science & Technology Park and will be able to seek the past achievement and current development in practical manner under one roof.

To mark the 30th Anniversary of NERD Centre, we have laid the foundation stone in 2004 for construction of NERDC Engineering Museum in which the engineering and technological products and processes designed by ancient Sri Lankan people will be installed in the immediate future. Presently, the construction of the museum building is in progress. Our engineers and scientists are engaged in making interactive exhibits to be installed for the museum. In addition, some of the engineering equipments and models are to be purchased from the foreign countries. Once we complete the construction of museum, we would be able to install models depicting ancient Technologies like Bisokotuwa, Sekkuwa etc. and other engineering models in order to uplift the science, technology and engineering knowledge of the people.

Results and Discussion

Past Achievements:

Table II–Visitors to park in groups in year 2005

Month	*School Groups*	*Other Institution*	*Total*
January	2	2	4
February	6	5	11
March	23	8	31
April	5	4	9
May	18	12	30
June	20	10	30
July	44	13	57
August	32	14	46
September	20	5	25
October	19	6	25
November	4	3	7
December	8	8	16

Table III–Visitors to park in groups in year 2004

Month	*School Groups*	*Other Institution*	*Total*
January	-	2	2
February	7	3	10
March	21	4	25
April	3	1	4
May	15	10	25
June	18	10	28
July	47	6	53
August	35	11	46
September	15	5	20
October	22	8	30
November	14	9	23
December	5	6	11

Table IV–Visitors to park in groups in year 2003

Month	*School Group*	*Other Institution*	*Total*
January	3	2	5
February	15	2	17
March	34	4	38
April	21	4	25
May	12	1	13
June	17	2	19
July	51	6	57
August	20	4	24
September	18	3	21
October	19	7	26
November	6	5	11
December	4	3	7
Total	**220**	**43**	**263**

Table V–Visitors to park in groups in year 2002

Month	*School Groups*	*Other Institution*	*Total*
January	-	5	5
February	7	2	9
March	37	3	40
April	22	5	27
May	13	2	15
June	37	4	41
July	42	3	45
August	22	11	33
September	18	2	20
October	21	7	28
November	8	3	11
December	3	1	4
Total	186	38	224

According to the data collected, visitors to the Technology Park have increased annually. At the same time, the number of groups and other institutions that visited the park have increased (see tables). The current year, the visitors arrival has been decreased due to the presidential election which was held to elect new president to the Sri Lanka. This increase is mainly through word of mouth from visitors without the attempts made through the advertisement. Our services to the visitors are through the lectures by our demonstrators and Technical Staff. Practical demonstrations are carried out and science concepts are taught. At the same time the visitors are coming to the Technology Park to gather information regarding the projects for their educational reports.

Conclusions

People have thirst for science. They are eager to learn more about science. People are learning everyday and improve their knowledge. Specially in a third world developing country like Sri Lanka, there are talent, skilled youngsters and students who can create innovative/ inventive things, if they could learn science & technological concepts in practical manner during their learning process. To make creative people, the government as well as intellectuals should be able to make a national policy regarding the setting up of the museums as well as science and technological Centres throughout the country to popularize the science among the people. Then the people will be able to apply the practical experience gained through these Centres in order to apply these skills to live in this world better.

Acknowledgements

Any project which is carried out at any level, is a result of coordination and assimilation of work done by number of individual experts and institutions without which even to think of its completion may be compared to any dream.

Before acknowledging due helps at different levels from different persons, I would like to mention the main inspiration behind the work in the name of the Chairman of NERDC Mr. Jayantha Ranathunga for his cooperation and encouragement during the moments in which it seemed nearly impossible for me to complete the work.

My respected General Manager Mr. M.W.Leelaratne came out with his valuable instructions and suggestions from time to time for which I am very grateful to him.

I would like to acknowledge with sincere regards the help rendered to me by Deputy General Manager (Services) Mr.D.C.Jayaratne who was never short of giving help of any kind during my work. I am also thankful to Mr.W.R.Sowis, Mrs. P.D.R.Damayanthi and Mr. K.A.J.Perera in Technology Park for their assistance.

Last but not the least, my dear wife Bhadra and sons Shanaka, Kovida, Miyuru and Navoda and daughter Achini are the ones who count much more than anyone.

References

- www.a-zoftourism.com
- www.namstct.org
- www.srilankatourism.org/museums.htm

Abbreviations

NERDC	-	National Engineering Research and Development Centre
S&T	-	Science and Technology

Status of Museums in Zambia: Are Museums Mirrors or Warehouses

Mudenda George S
Director
Lusaka National Museum, ZAMBIA

Introduction

Culture distinguishes people from other creatures. E.A. Hoebel argues that, "human beings are unique among all the creatures of the animal kingdom in their capacity to create and sustain culture. Each society of people possesses its own distinctive culture, so that the members of one society behave differently in some significant respects from the members of every other society". Culture therefore, can be defined as the integrated sum of learned behaviour traits, which are manifested and shared by the members of a society. It may further be thought of as a social heritage for it is handed down by percept from one new generation to another.

The conference themes reflect broader intellectual shifts in the ways in which the role of science and museums is understood. The purpose of this paper is to explore the conference theme on "The Enhanced Role of Science Centers and Museums in Development Strategies". This paper is aimed at highlighting the need to consider museums as mirrors rather than warehouses in developing strategies in science and development. It is organized in two parts. **Part I** focuses on issues pertaining to role of museums. While **Part II** attempts to sketch country status of museums and the application of science in these institutions.

Part I: The Role of Museums

Operational definition

A museum is viewed as an institution that helps people understand the world by using objects and ideas to interpret the past and present and explore the future. A museum preserves collections and researches, and makes objects and information accessible in actual and virtual environments. Museums are established in the public interest as permanent, non-profit making organizations that contribute long-term value to communities. In this aspect a museum is viewed to be a custodian of people's culture including that of the local communities.

Role of Museums in Developing Strategies

It is important to ask questions like "Is a museum a mirror or repository (Warehouse)? This then should bring us to the role of the museum in a scientific environment. In the recent years, construction and mounting of exhibitions with a scientific bias by both museum professionals and local communities to represent their own cultures have become a flourishing phenomenon in countries all over the world. On the wave of this kind of movement, there has been a growing trend in most museums housing peoples' cultures around the world to mount exhibitions on social cultures in most African countries - Zambia inclusive. This is mainly done with the representatives of the subject culture so as to provide them with opportunities to exhibit their own cultures. This stems from the idea that museums are repositories rather than the ultimate mirrors of science development stages through the objects/artifacts collected. A mirror shows how you appear after wearing a new pair of clothing or having taken a shower. This means the focal agenda of museum exhibitions and programmes alike should be to reflect the scientific progression of any society from its infancy levels of technology to the higher ones. Furthermore they need to indicate the factors at play. As far as enhanced role of museums in developing strategies is concerned, exhibitions are an important step to mirror the science development of a society or nation. In view of this one may refer to the role of the museum as that of being a forum, thus a place promoting multidirectional social and scientific development. A museum is a place where the hosts of the exhibition (museum), the people viewing the exhibitions (audience) and the people exhibited (those whose scientific technology is represented) interact and learn from each other.

Professor Yoshida in quoting Cameron writes that museums have choices in either becoming temples or forums. A museum as a **temple** is a place where people come to worship "treasures" with pre-established values. The museum as a **forum** is a place where people can have an encounter with the unknown, which generates a discussion and debate. Professor Yoshida further argues that the forum is where battles are fought while the temple is where the victors rest. The former is a process while the latter is a product. The idea of a museum as a forum should therefore be conceptualized in enhancement of the role of museums in developing strategies.

It is also important at this stage to note that a museum exhibition is nothing more than a fragment of reality chosen from a certain viewpoint for a particular purpose. However, this does not mean that there is no substance which is represented in the exhibition. It simply shows the early stages of the scientific development. When Yoshida said a museum is a forum where battles are fought he meant that the museums should take upon themselves contradictions, conflicts and difficulties faced in every day life in development of scientific environment.

Part II: Status of Museums in Zambia

Zambia as a nation has four national and two privately owned museums dotted around the country. There is Copperbelt Museum in Ndola, Livingstone Museum in Livingstone, Lusaka National Museum in Lusaka, and Moto Moto Museum in Mbala. Livingstone Museum is the biggest in both establishment and collection, followed by Moto Moto Museum and the Copperbelt and Lusaka National Museums. Nayuma in Mongu, Western Province and the Choma Museum and Crafts Centre in Choma, Southern Province are the two privately owned museums.

The four national museums fall under the National Museums Board of Zambia (NMB), which was established in 1966 by an Act of Parliament CAP 174 of the Laws of Zambia. The National Museums Board is a government grant-aided body in the Ministry of Tourism, Environment and Natural Resources.

NMB Mission

"To establish, manage and develop National Museums on a sustainable basis for the preservation and interpretation of movable heritage for the benefit of the present and future generations". This means that the NMB manages all national museums in Zambia. The core functions of the museums are to exhibit, manage and develop staff, research, collect, collection management, document collections, conduct public programmes, rehabilitate and develop museums buildings.

Museums and Science

In this turbulent sea of change, the National Museums Board has undertaken drastic measures in the enhancement of the role of museums in development strategies. Bearing the complexities of the subject of science and technology the NMB assigned themes to its respective museum entities in 1996 through the restructuring process. These themes ranged from Cultural History to Natural History. This meant that each museum was to expand according to its theme and this is the current scenario in most of the NMB museums.

As a measure for the national museums to become centres connecting individuals and families as well as offering the opportunity to raise awareness of current research and stimulating an interest in science, NMB has proposed the establishment of the Museum of Science and Technology in Ndola. This will be independent of the current existing Copperbelt Museum. The museum exhibits will:

- Make exploring science and technology a relevant, exciting and meaningful learning experience for children and adults.
- Become important source of informal science education for the community.
- Contain real objects and phenomena, specimen and samples, supported by models, maps, photos, multimedia and words to create a memorable and motivating visitor experience – an experience that will present visitors with a diversity of Copperbelt's and Africa's participation in and connection to science and technology with special focus on the history of geology and mining.
- Focus primarily on Copperbelt using regional examples to illustrate concepts and geological principles with reference to national and global examples where applicable.
- Underscore the impact of science and technology on society and people's everyday lives.
- Connect the public to the museum's public programming initiatives, research science around the world and other disciplines such as archaeology and history.

The project has so far held two stakeholders' workshops, which were designed to develop themes of the new museum, type of collections, space utilization, types of exhibitions and many other considerations. The current status of this project is that a team of professionals drawn from museums and other non-museum institutions are conducting a feasibility study.

In an effort to make museums become special nexus among community, the school and the home, Lusaka National Museum provides special science related public programmes that can propel science education and other development reforms. Notable programmes include "They Lived Science". This programme started in 2004 and it centered on the premises of position of Science and Technology in cultural artefacts. The programme had the following objectives at its inception:

- Develop a framework to analyse cultural artefacts to determine their scientific, mathematical and technological principles.
- Promote children's awareness of the educational importance of cultural objects as they could contribute to their scientific, mathematical and technological learning.
- Design an interactive exhibition of selected artefacts that carry on board both children and adults as active learners of Science, Mathematics and Technology.
- Inculcate the appreciation of Science in children by making its application in cultural artefacts an entertainment experience.
- Create awareness to the general public to appreciate Science as part of the basic way of life.

In the year 2005 the programme placed emphasis on "Crafting Indigenous Fruit shells for Environmental

Sustainability". Our Education Officer conducted a research, followed by a workshop with school children which culminated into an exhibition. This was done in collaboration with MIAPEN Zambia Crafts and the Commonwealth Forestry Association, Zambia.

The Livingstone Museum holds the largest natural history collection in the country, including mammals, birds, insects, reptiles, amphibians, fish and plants. The mammal and bird collections which dates back to the 1960s, the insect, reptile and amphibian collections began in the 1970s, while the fish and plant sections are quite new and are in the process of being built up. The collections are preserved in store rooms as reference material for scientific research.

The Natural History Department carries out research in the above fields, particularly in the areas of taxonomy and ecology, although limited funding has hindered these activities considerably over the past decade. The Museum has permanent public exhibitions on natural science topics including balance of life, food chains, natural cycles, insects, birds, amphibians, reptiles, plants, fish, mammals, environment and pollution. Temporary exhibitions on various topics are put up from time to time.

Talks, film shows and slide shows on various wildlife and environmental topics are given to school groups and clubs on request. Members of staff occasionally assist high school pupils with their JETS projects where they relate to museum fields.

The Department takes part in animal censuses, such as the African Waterfowl Census, which is conducted biannually, and censuses of large mammals in the nearby Mosi-o-tunya National Park.

Lusaka National Museum has conducted Food Fairs involving women from Zambia's nine provinces to promote nutritionally rich traditional food. The idea is to promote local food so that the majority of the population can obtain nutrition without resorting to exotic foodstuffs.

Limitations

- Limited funding from Government
- Limited and inadequate storage facilities for collections
- Lack of transport for educational outreach activities
- Lack of adequate transport and funding for research activities

Moto Moto Museum has a small number of natural history collections, which range from insects, mammals, birds, fish, amphibians to reptiles.

In all museums, however, the situation is made difficult by the fact that promotion of science development is taking place slowly due to none availability of human, financial, material and institutional resources which are inadequate to handle the progress.

Conclusion

The discussion in this paper has highlighted the role museums play in the development of science and technology. It is therefore necessary to encompass them in national development strategies of science. To enhance the role of museums there is need to build a trans-disciplinary approach where institutions such as National Science Centre and Centre for Science and Technology of the Non-Aligned and other Developing Countries work together with museum. To foster trans-disciplinary approach, it is recommendable that comparative research and co-operation exits between local and international science centres and museums.

There is urgent need for an initiative to explore a potentially expanded role for museums so that they can effectively play the role in development strategies of each country. The centrepiece of museum roles in the first place may consist of a series of dialogues, each envisioned as a focused "laboratory" involving people who are concerned with the day-to-day business of linking communities and museums. As a consequence of the role museums play, the public will experience exhibitions that explore folk culture, science, technology and other natural and social phenomena of human development.

The Enhanced Role of Science Centres and Museums in Development Strategies

African Regional Conference
10–14 January 2006, Lusaka, Zambia

A BRIEF REPORT

Science is a part of our culture and society, and science centres and science museums provide a distinctive networking between the community, the school and the home giving them a unique role in the educational infrastructure. In view of the immense importance attached by the NAM S&T Centre to science centres and science museums in the society and development, an international workshop was organised by the Centre focusing on 'The Role of Science Centres in Development Strategies' in Kolkata, India during Nov-Dec 2002. At the conclusion of this workshop a Kolkata Declaration was adopted, emphasising on holding a general workshop on science centers for all developing countries once every alternate year and a regional workshop during the intervening period. In pursuance thereof, the Centre in partnership with the Maloka Science Centre of Colombia organised the 1st Knowledge Fest and 2nd International Forum and Workshop on 'Culture of Science, Technology and Innovation in Society' in Bogotá, Colombia during March 24-26, 2004 as a regional workshop for the Latin American and Caribbean countries. Subsequently, the Centre held an international workshop on the theme 'The Changing role of Science Centres and Museums in

Developing Countries' on October 20-22, 2004 in Hanoi in collaboration with the Center for Regional Research & Development (CRD), Ministry of Science & Technology of Vietnam.

With the approval of its Governing Council, the NAM S&T Centre, jointly with the National Science Centre, Zambia, organised the African Regional Conference on 'Enhanced Role of Science Centres and Museums in Developmental Strategies' at Lusaka during 10-14 January 2006. The workshop was, among others, aimed at proposing strategies for the formulation and application of programmes and projects for the development of a culture of science, technology and innovation, bringing together the science popularisation experts and museologists to share their knowledge and ideas about the role of science centres and museums in development strategies and the benefits to society, and sustainable development by better exploitation of science centres and museums through communication and media.

Mr. Gaston Chola, Deputy Minister of Education of Zambia inaugurated the workshop after the opening remarks from Prof. Arun P. Kulshreshtha, Director, NAM S&T Centre, Mr. Michelo D. B. Hakasenke, Director, Teacher Education and Specialised Services and Mr. Festus Hang'andu Mungo, Chief Education Officer - Specialised Services of Zambia of the Ministry of Education, Zambia.

Twenty five scientists and senior experts from 8 countries, which included Angola [Mr. Emmanuel Jeronimo Jaime João Chitende, Angolan Embassy in Zambia], Botswana [Mrs. Gloria Tiny Seitei, Senior Communications Officer, Botswana Technology Centre, Gaborone], India [Dr. Tapan K. Ganguly, Director, Science City, Kolkata and Dr. Abhay Kothari, Manthan, Ahmedabad], Japan [Mr. Hideo Nakano, Senior Volunteer, JICA], Pakistan [Dr.

Mrs. Alia Bano Munshi, Principal Scientific Officer, PCSIR Complex, Karachi], South Africa [Dr. Richard Waller, Greenhouse Management Services, Johannesburg and Mr. Alfred Tsipa, President SAASTEC and Manager, Unizul Science Centre, Empangeni], Sri Lanka [Mr. Arumahennadige Piyasiri, Mechanical Engineer, National Engineering Research and Development Centre, Ja-ela] and Zambia [Mr. John S. Muyangana, Principal Education Officer, Mrs. Hilda L. Nyemba, Mr. Donald K. Mwaba and Mr. James M. Chongo, Senior Education Officer and other officials of the National Science Centre. Mr. George S. Mudenda, Director, Lusaka National Museum; and Mr. Lloyd S. Thole from the Ministry of Science, Technology and Vocational Training (MSTV) also attended the regional conference. They presented status papers on the activities related to the science centres and museums in their countries.

Dr. Paul Zambezi, Permanent Secretary, MSTV, who is also the Focal Point person for the NAM S&T Centre in Zambia, gave a talk at the end of the technical sessions. Visits were organised to the National Science Centre (NSC) of Zambia and the Lusaka Museum. The visit at the NSC highlighted among other projects the development of the Science Park where, so far, three exhibits are in place. The other aspect of the NSC showed the effort they are making in promoting the teaching of science and technology subjects by the production of various teaching aids.

The concluding session was devoted to the discussion on preparing recommendations for the governments of the developing countries and use by the relevant agencies, after which the Certificates of Participation were awarded to the participants by Mr. M. D. B. Hakasenke, Director, Teacher Education and Specialised Services of Zambia. The final recommendations are appended to this report.

The foreign participants also took this opportunity to visit the magnificent Victoria Falls at Livingstone situated about 500 km south of Lusaka bordering with Zimbabwe and the Science Museum in Livingstone town.

LUSAKA RECOMMENDATIONS 2006

An international regional conference on Science Centres and Museums was organised in Lusaka, Zambia from 10-14 January 2006 with an objective of bringing together science popularization experts and museologists to share knowledge and ideas about the role of science centres and museums in development strategies and the benefits of society. The participants in the conference included the experts and museologists from Angola, Botswana, India, Japan, Pakistan, South Africa, Sri Lanka and Zambia. The conference emphasised the need to equip our people with scientific learning and thinking skills.

The deliberations of the conference ended with the following recommendations:

- Realising that science centers and museums are very strong vehicle for popularization of science among the common people and are very useful tool for supplementing curriculum teaching in science in schools and colleges, the participants recommended that every African country which does not have a science centre or a museum in the country may seriously consider the establishment of such institutions, and in doing so, may seek the assistance of other countries that have already succeeded in this direction.Realising that science centres and museums are very strong vehicle for popularisation of science among the common people and are very useful tool for supplementing curriculum teaching in science in schools and colleges, the participants recommended that every African country which does not have a science centre or a museum in the country may seriously consider the establishment of such institutions, and in doing so, may seek the assistance of other countries that have already succeeded in this direction.

- There is urgent need for an initiative to explore a potentially expanded role for science centres and museums so that they can effectively play their role in development strategies of each country.
- The participants urged the Governments of all the developing countries to strengthen their commitment to the reinforcement of science and museums through increased funding and support.The participants urged the Governments of all the developing countries to strengthen their commitment to the reinforcement of science centres and museums through increased funding and support.
- It was proposed that subject to its internal formalities, SAASTEC from Southern Africa may join the NAM S&T Centre as its S&T-Industry member.
- It was proposed that SAASTEC investigate cooperation strategies with the appropriate organisations in India, which has the largest network of science centres in the NAM countries.
- There is need to upgrade the National Science Centre of Zambia to a fully-fledged entity, which will help in spreading science popularization within the country.
- Local and international partnerships among individual institutions should be promoted through networking and

further there is need to extend this to other centres and institutions.

- It is recommended that science centres and museums, which have private partnerships, are allowed to be legally structured to afford tax relief to private sector benefactors.
- The next international conference on science centres and museums may be organised by the NAM S&T Centre in association with a competent agency once again in an African country, or a country in the Middle Eastern / Arab regions.

The Enhanced Role of Science Centres and Museums in Development Strategies

African Regional Conference
10–14 January 2006, Lusaka, Zambia

List of Participants

Ms. Gloria Seitei
Botswana Technology Centre,
Botswana.
Phone: 267 3914161
Fax: 267 3974467
E-mail: Gloria@botec.bw

Mr. Abhay Kothari
Manthan Educational Programme Society
Ahemdabad,
India
Phone: 91 79-26766571
91 9825062409
E-mail: manthan@sify.com

Dr. T.K. Ganguly
Director,
Science City, Kolkata,
India
Phone: 91-33-23441818
Fax: 91-33-22859895
E-mail: sctycal@cal.vsnl.net.in

Mr. Nikola Risk Guirgues
General Director,
City of Science,
Academy of Scientific Research and Technology (ASRT),
Egypt
Phone: 202 7921305 (O)
202 4451153 (R)
Fax: 202 7921305
E-mail: rizknikola@yahoo.com

Dr. Alia Munshi
Principal Scientific Officer
Pakistan Council for Scientific and Industrial Research, Lahore,
Pakistan
Phone: 92-21-4659785 (O)
92-21-2255094 (R)
E-mail: munshi5@cyber.net.pk

Dr. Richard Waller
Consultant
Greenhouse Management Services (PTY) LTD
Block D, Carlon Falco Office Park, 16 Southway, Kelvin
Johannesburg
South Africa
Phone: 27 11 444 7117
Fax: 27 11 444 7225
E-mail: rwaller@greenhouse.co.za

Mr. Alfred Tsipa
President,
SAASTEC
South Africa
Phone: 27 35 79 73 204
E-mail: atsipa@iafrica.com

Mr. Piyasiri Arumahennadige
Engineer-in-Charge (NERDC Technology Park),
National Engineering Research & Development Centre,
Sri Lanka
Phone: 94-11-2236384
94-11-2845653
Fax: 94-11-2236434
E-mail: nerdcentre@nerdc.lk, techno@nerdc.lk

Mr. George S. Mudenda
Director,
Lusaka National Museum,
Zambia
Phone: 260-1-223788
E-mail: lusamus@zamnet.zm, gmudenda@yahoo.co.uk

Mr. Gaston Chola
Deputy Minister,
Ministery of Education,
PO Box 50093,
Zambia
Phone: 260-1-250855
E-mail: gchola@moe.gov.zm

Mr. Michelo D. B. Hakasenke
Director,
Teacher Education and Specialised Services,
Zambia
Phone: 260-1-250162
E-mail: mdbhakasenke@moe.gov.zm

Mr. Festus Hang' Andu Mungo
Chief Education Officer,
Specialised Services,
Zambia
Phone: 260-1-256550
E-mail: fmungo@moe.gov.zm

Dr. Paul Zambezi
Permanent Secretary,
Ministry of Science, Technology and Vocational Training,
Post Box No. 50464,
Lusaka, Zambia
Phone: 260-1-252411
E-mail: paulzam2002@yahoo.com

Mrs. Hilda L. Nyemba
Senior Education Officer (Science),
National Science Centre,
Zambia
Phone: 260-1-263391
260-97-683713
E-mail: nyemba2001@yahoo.com

Mr. Habeenzu Chilala
Assistant Curator,
Lusaka National Museum,
Zambia
Phone: 260-1-228806
260-97-704223
E-mail: chilalahabenzu@yahoo.com, lusamus@zamnet.zm

Mr. Yvonne Mulala
Assistant Education Officer,
Lusaka National Museum,
Zambia
Phone: 260-1-228806
260-97-416785
E-mail: myruwe@hotmail.com

Mr. Jack Chishala
Chairperson,
Zambia Association for Technology Education,
Zambia
Phone: 260-1-26339, 260-1-227710
260-97-851561
E-mail: chishalajack@yahoo.co.uk

Dr. Donald K. Mwaba
Senior Education Officer (Metal and Electrical),
National Science Centre,
Zambia
Phone: 260-1-263391
260-1-250076
260-97-845382
260-95-833195
E-mail: dmwaba2002@yahoo.co.uk

Mr. James M. Chongo
JICA Senior Volunteer,
National Science Centre,
Zambia
Phone: 260-1-263391
260-97-439480
260-97-165333
E-mail: chongojames@yahoo.co.uk

Mr. Hideo Nakano
Senior Education Officer (Wood and Plastic),
National Science Centre,
Zambia
Phone: 260-1-263391
E-mail: nhl886@yahoo.co.jp

Mr. John S. Muyangana
Principal Education Officer,
National Science Centre,
Zambia
Phone: 260-1-263391
260-97-106216
260-95-819925
E-mail: johnmuyangana@yahoo.com

Mr. Leonard K. Shampile
Acting Chief Curriculum Specialist,
CDC,
Zambia
Phone: 260-1-254848
260-95-915776
E-mail: leonardshampile@yahoo.com

Mr. Ruth Chirwa
Secretary,
National Science Centre,
Zambia
Phone: 260-1-263391
260-95-827887
260-96-587387
E-mail: ruthchirwa@yahoo.com, nsczamtel.zm

Mr. Chanda Dorothy Kasanda
Secretary,
TESS,
Zambia
Phone: 260-1-256550
260-97-1633532
E-mail: dochaka2004@yahoo.co.uk

Prof. Arun P. Kulshreshtha
Director,
NAM S&T Centre
New Delhi,
India
Phone: 91 11 24644974
91 11 24645134
Fax: 91 11 24644973
E-mail: namstct@gmail.com, apknam@gmail.com